T0243247

PRAISE FOR
THE SUSTAINABLE BUSINESS BOOK

"Vital for anyone wanting to galvanize genuinely sustainable change in their business."

ZOE BALE
Senior Client Lead, Channel 4

"Love it. The PLANET System is great and gives a structure to how leaders can approach their thinking and action on this tricky topic."

RICHARD BRADFORD
Human Resources Director, Dentsu International

"Love the PLANET System – so smart."

JAMILA BROWN
Head of House Foundations, Soho House

"The framework will help navigate and develop much-needed actions that could change the PLANET. Every marketer needs this book in their back pocket at all times."

GEMMA BUTLER
Co-author, *Sustainable Marketing: How to Drive Profits with Purpose*

FOR OTHER TITLES
IN THE SERIES...

CONCISE
ADVICE
LAB

SMALL
BOOKS:
BIG
IDEAS

CLEVER CONTENT, DYNAMIC IDEAS, PRACTICAL
SOLUTIONS AND ENGAGING VISUALS –
A CATALYST TO INSPIRE NEW WAYS OF THINKING
AND PROBLEM-SOLVING IN A COMPLEX WORLD

lidpublishing.com/books/concise-advice

Published by
LID Publishing
An imprint of LID Business Media Ltd.
LABS House, 15-19 Bloomsbury Way,
London, WC1A 2TH, UK

info@lidpublishing.com
www.lidpublishing.com

A member of:

businesspublishersroundtable.com

Printed by Imak Ofset

ISBN: 978-1-911687-80-1 (paperback)
ISBN: 978-1-911687-40-5 (hardback)
ISBN: 978-1-911687-41-2 (ebook)

Cover and page design: Caroline Li

THE SUSTAINABLE BUSINESS BOOK

BUILDING A RESILIENT MODERN BUSINESS IN SIX STEPS

KEVIN DUNCAN
SARAH DUNCAN

MADRID | MEXICO CITY | LONDON
BUENOS AIRES | BOGOTA | SHANGHAI

CONTENTS

LIST OF FIGURES

FOREWORD

It's never fun to start with the doom and gloom. But sometimes you just can't avoid it. The truth is, we're in a crisis. The science is clear: we must keep the global temperature rise below 1.5°C (vs global temperatures before the Industrial Revolution) if we want to avoid the most catastrophic effects of the climate crisis. To do that, we urgently need to slash our greenhouse gas emissions: by half by 2030 and to zero by 2050.

The good news is that we have everything we need to get there. Other crises we've faced recently, such as the Covid-19 pandemic, have shown us that we *can* come together collectively to tackle these crises. The hard bit will actually be doing it, and that's where we need willpower. The climate crisis is no longer a technological problem – it's a people problem. Which means that solving it requires every part of society – especially businesses – to take urgent action.

If you're intimidated by that idea, you're not alone. I've witnessed first hand the trials and tribulations that come with trying to balance a sustainability agenda with traditional corporate pressures. And I can tell you that many businesses don't get it right. But it is the ones that do that are truly resilient – standing out among the competition, attracting and keeping brilliant talent, and much more.

These businesses are the ones that can keep thinking long term in the midst of short-term pressures. This is difficult – our brains are hardwired to prioritize the here and now. But that's where this fantastic new book can help. The revolutionary PLANET System will break down complex issues into easily digestible steps that you can take right now. There's no daunting science – just enough data to inform you and help you to take action.

The important thing is to get going because we really don't have time to waste. Businesses caused many of the world's most pressing issues – it's time they solved them.

This is *our* crisis. No matter what business we are in, we must all get involved.

Shaunagh Duncan, Head of Sustainability UK & Benelux, Oatly

INTRODUCTION

Building a resilient modern business involves a delicate balance between being commercially savvy and being operationally responsible. It's a constant juggling act.

If you want to get to grips with the sustainability agenda and apply it properly to your company, you are going to need a proper system rather than a haphazard series of well-intentioned but half-baked initiatives.

That's why we invented the PLANET System®. Follow it and you will make progress. This sort of improvement does not come about by chance. It requires dedication, proper resources and consistency.

The system is informed by a large amount of research, reading and consulting over the past six years. We have also been through the complete process of B Corp certification ourselves, which has helped to shine a light on our own business and make sure that we practice what we preach.

We have deliberately written this book in such a way that you should be able to implement the system on your own. If you have any difficulty in doing so, please get in touch and we will try to help. If you work in a large organization and would like additional assistance, let us know and we will guide you through the process with structured workshops and consultancy. More details on this and other products at sustainablebusinessbook.com.

Knowing that this is also very much a generational issue, we decided to ask a potential CEO of the future who knows a lot about sustainability to give her perspective as a thirty-year-old. She also happens to be our daughter. Read her thoughts in the foreword.

Kevin and Sarah Duncan
Westminster, 2023

THE PLANET SYSTEM®

Before all this talk of sustainability, we had CSR – corporate social responsibility. This was a long-standing approach to doing the right thing, but it centred mainly on waiting to see what profit was generated in a year and then distributing some of it to good causes. It was something of an afterthought to the central business model.

Forward-thinking, sustainable businesses now harness responsible behaviour as an integral part of generating profit. Ethical behaviour for these companies is therefore built into the core of the business.

This new approach builds moral purpose into the company at the beginning of the financial year, not the end.

The term 'ESG' has now widely taken over from CSR. ESG stands for *environmental, social and governance*.

The terms 'ESG' and 'sustainability' are broadly interchangeable. Many people still associate sustainability more with environmental matters or a green agenda, but, as we will reiterate many times in this book, sustainable development covers **the planet *and* people**. ESG seems to command more attention in a corporate context – particularly the inclusion of good governance – although you would think that this should be a given, particularly in more regulated sectors.

We don't think it matters which term you use. ESG will no doubt evolve into some other trending acronym. Just avoid getting tied up by word definitions rather than getting on with improving your company's business operations.

> Ultimately, it's about how your actions, products or services contribute to (or detract from) a healthy planet and a healthy society.

Sustainability in the true sense of the word means 'to endure.' In this context, we are talking about you and your company.

Too many businesspeople think that sustainability is just "the environmental stuff" or "the green stuff." It certainly does include these critical issues, but it is much, much more than that.

Reducing sustainability to a single (usually green) issue disguises its complexity in an unhelpful way. This is sometimes referred to as *carbon tunnel vision* (see over).

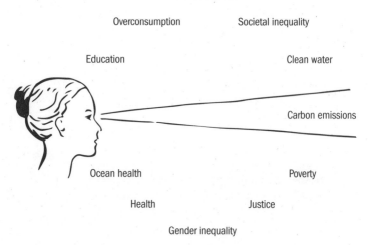

Biodiversity loss

Overconsumption

Societal inequality

Education

Clean water

Carbon emissions

Ocean health

Poverty

Health

Justice

Gender inequality

A modern, smart, ethical business that wants to trade successfully in the future needs to attend to a great number of serious issues and juggle many themes simultaneously.

OUR DEFINITION OF BUSINESS SUSTAINABILITY

The creation or reengineering of a company to be successful while doing as little harm as possible.

This is not just 'the environmental stuff.' It means looking after people and acknowledging societal issues, such as social injustice and inequality, as well as prioritizing the decarbonization of business operations, reducing waste, and preserving and replenishing natural resources.

All of this requires a multifaceted approach, which isn't easy. You need a system (*Figure 1*).

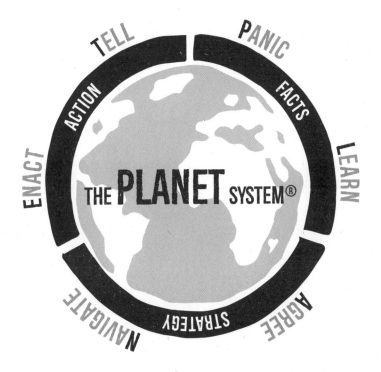

FIGURE 1 – The PLANET System®

The PLANET System® is a registered UK trademark of Expert Advice Limited and held at the Intellectual Property Office in the United Kingdom, Trade Mark No: UK 00003781373.

The PLANET System is carefully structured to help guide businesses through the process of becoming more sustainable. There are three stages and six steps to follow.

The three stages are:
1. **FACTS**
2. **STRATEGY**
3. **ACTION**

Each stage involves two steps, as follows:

STAGE 1: FACTS

 Panic   **Step One:** *Confront the issues directly*

 Learn   **Step Two:** *Get properly informed*

STAGE 2: STRATEGY

Agree   **Step Three:** *Decide your strategic direction*

Navigate   **Step Four:** *Overcome obstacles*

STAGE 3: ACTION

Enact   **Step Five:** *Get it done*

Tell   **Step Six:** *Communicate with integrity*

STEP ONE. *Confront the issues directly.* A company that doesn't realize how serious the problem is needs to **PANIC**. That means shaking things up, putting your business under the sustainability spotlight and getting everyone to realize that they need to put the subject at the top of the agenda. Even if awareness of sustainability issues is broadly high, the *PLANET System ESG Audit* (see 1.5) will give you a tangible framework for future improvement.

STEP TWO. *Get properly informed.* After that it is important to fill in the gaps in your knowledge: what do you need to **LEARN** about and understand before you formulate a full plan? This may well involve admitting what you don't know and finding out more, and becoming comfortable with technical information so as to avoid superficial conversations.

STEP THREE. *Decide your strategic direction.* Then comes one of the hardest parts: getting everyone to **AGREE**. Companies are riddled with disagreement – rifts in boards, those who are resistant to change, those who keep worrying about money while ignoring what is the right thing to do. Few meetings end with a unanimous decision. So it is crucial that a strategic direction is clearly decided upon, without any room for misunderstanding, and that everyone signs up to it. That's the role of the *Improvement Plan* (see 3.5).

STEP FOUR. *Overcome obstacles.* It is important to work out what all the obstacles to progress are. All companies have them, whether they are organizational, financial, structural or simply from individuals not agreeing or refusing to change their behaviour. The ability to **NAVIGATE** through all this requires intelligent planning, some inevitable sacrifices and more honesty from all decision-makers. All the details of this will be brought to the surface with tools to help prioritize tasks and overcome resistance.

STEP FIVE. *Get it done.* Of course, it is essential to **ENACT** the plan. This is always easier said than done. It requires constant effort and, most importantly, getting your attitude right. For sustainable thinking to be truly embedded in a company, it needs to become part of the core or culture of the business, not just a side project.

STEP SIX. *Communicate with integrity.* Finally, all of this work needs to be communicated authentically and intelligently to anyone who will listen – you need to **TELL** all your stakeholders, including employees, shareholders, suppliers and customers. This stage should only be deployed when genuine improvements have been made. These improvements will manifest themselves in an *Impact Report* (see 6.5), which needs to be reviewed constantly and communicated with integrity.

STAGE 1

FACTS

STEP ONE – PANIC
CONFRONT THE
ISSUES DIRECTLY

The P of the PLANET System stands for **PANIC**.

Companies need to realize how serious the problem is. They need to understand the severity and urgency surrounding sustainability.

That means facing uncomfortable facts, asking awkward questions and putting the subject at the top of the agenda.

This stage provides the backdrop to the whole process, briefs you on all the important sustainability issues and introduces the *PLANET System ESG Audit* – a series of questions you can use to assess the current state of your business.

STEP ONE

PANIC

Infinite growth on a planet with finite resources is unsustainable. We are living beyond our means.

Paul Gilding, Environmentalist

1.1. INFINITE GROWTH, FINITE PLANET

The earth has entered a new age – the Anthropocene – where humans are now the most dominant species and have the most powerful influence on our environment and our climate (*Economics for a Fragile Planet*, Edward Barbier).

Since the mid-20th century, the world has experienced explosive population growth (from 2.7 billion in 1955 to nearly 8 billion in 2022). This has created unprecedented demand and caused the deterioration of the natural resources needed to fuel and support this growth. This rapid acceleration of progress (plus resource deterioration) is known as the *Great Acceleration*.

Here are some facts on the depletion of the world's natural resources and our current overconsumption.

- Humanity currently uses the equivalent of 1.7 planets to provide the resources necessary to provide goods and absorb waste. (*Global Footprint Network 2018*)

1.7 planets
needed

- We have created over 170,000 synthetic mineral-like substances, such as plastic, concrete, steel, ceramics and artificial drugs, against around just 5,000 natural minerals.

170,000
Synthetic substances

vs

5,000
Natural minerals

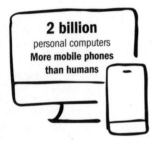

2 billion
personal computers
**More mobile phones
than humans**

- There are now 1.4 billion motor vehicles, 2 billion personal computers and more mobile phones than people on earth. (*How to Save Our Planet*, Mark Maslin)

- We extract over 80 million tons of seafood from our oceans every year and have reduced 30% of fish stocks to critical levels.

80 billion
tons of seafood extracted

15 billion
trees cut down

- We cut down 15 billion trees a year. The top driver of deforestation is beef production.

- 70% of the mass of birds on the planet are domesticated – mainly chickens (we eat 50 billion each year). 96% of the mass of all animals on earth is of those we raise to eat. (*A Life on Our Planet*, David Attenborough)

50 billion
chickens eaten

This rapid growth has also put extreme pressure on our social foundations.

- In 2017, the world's richest 1% of adults owned 50.1% of global wealth. (Credit Suisse, 2017)

50.1%
of global wealth belongs to richest
1%
of adults

Richest **42** adults possess same wealth as the poorest **50%** of world population

- In 2017, the world's richest 42 adults possessed the same wealth as the poorest 50% of the world's population. (Credit Suisse, 2017)

- The richest 20% of the population consumes close to 75.6% of all global resources, with the poorest 20% consuming a mere 1.5%. (Jupiter, 2016)

75.6%
by the richest 20%

Global resources consumed

1.5%
by the poorest 20%

Inequality emerged as a central issue for the Sustainable Development Goals because of the growing body of evidence that inequalities in income and wealth cause economic instability and a range of health and social problems, and create a roadblock to the adoption of pro-environment strategies and behaviour. Social and economic inequalities tear the social fabric, undermine social cohesion, contribute to environmental problems, and prevent nations, communities and individuals from flourishing. (*5 Reasons Why We Need to Reduce Global Inequality*, World Economic Forum)

ALL TALK, NO ACTION?
Do you and your company directors accept that resources are finite?

"

Right now, we are facing a man-made disaster of global scale. Our greatest threat in thousands of years. Climate change. If we don't take action, the collapse of our civilizations and the extinction of much of the natural world is on the horizon.

"

David Attenborough, *A Life on Our Planet*

1.2. CLIMATE CHANGE: A HOT TOPIC

The term *climate change* refers to long-term shifts in temperatures and weather patterns. These shifts may be natural, such as through variations in the solar cycle. But, most recently, human activities have been the main driver of climate change.

- Fossil fuels – coal, oil and gas – are by far the largest contributor to global climate change, accounting for over 75% of global greenhouse gas emissions and nearly 90% of all carbon dioxide emissions. As greenhouse gas emissions blanket the earth, they trap the sun's heat. This leads to global warming and climate change. The world is now warming faster than at any point in recorded history. Warmer temperatures over time are changing weather patterns and disrupting the usual balance of nature. This poses many risks to human beings and all other forms of life on earth. (*Causes and Effects of Climate Change*, United Nations)

- Greenhouse gases are at a 4.5 million-year high. Antarctica loses an Everest of ice every year. The homes of 200 million people will be below sea level in 70 years. Deserts are growing. Fires are becoming more frequent. Dangerous diseases are on the move. (*Facts that Bring Home the Reality of Climate Change*, National Geographic)

- The impacts of climate change will disrupt the natural, economic and social systems we depend on. This disruption will impact global food security, damage infrastructure and jobs, and harm human health. These impacts are unevenly distributed around the world, with some countries facing far greater risks than others. However, ALL countries, communities and companies will feel the effects of climate change. (Grantham Institute, Imperial College London)

- There are two numbers you need to know amount climate change: 51 billion is how many tons of greenhouse gases the world typically adds to the atmosphere every year. Zero is what we need to aim for to stop the warming and avoid the worst effects of climate change. There is no scenario in which we keep adding carbon to the atmosphere and the world stops getting hotter. The hotter it gets, the harder it will be for humans to survive, much less thrive. One fifth of carbon dioxide emitted today will still be there in 10,000 years. (*How to Avoid a Climate Disaster*, Bill Gates)

51 Billion

Zero

- We are not equally liable for the mess we find ourselves in. The richest 10% of the world's population emit 50% of carbon pollution into the atmosphere. The poorest 3.9 billion have contributed just 10%. (*How to Save Our Planet*, Mark Maslin)

- A 5-ton lifestyle is a suggested working target for the amount of CO_2e an average UK person should contribute per year. As it currently stands the 'average' global citizen has a footprint of 7 tons, with Americans at 21 tons, those in the UK at 13 tons and Malawians at 0.2 tons. (*How Bad Are Bananas?*, Mike Berners-Lee)

Average in America
21 Tons

Average in UK
13 Tons

Average in Malawi
0.2 Tons

A WORD ON CO$_2$

CO$_2$ is shorthand for *carbon dioxide*. It is one of the seven major greenhouse gases that contribute to climate change. Carbon dioxide exists naturally in the earth's atmosphere, but human activities since the Industrial Revolution have increased it to unsafe levels. More carbon dioxide in the atmosphere traps more heat that would otherwise be able to escape into space. It is this that has warmed our planet, causing climate change.

CO$_2$e is shorthand for *carbon dioxide equivalent*. This covers all greenhouse gas emissions that contribute to climate change, including carbon dioxide (CO$_2$), methane (CH$_4$), nitrous oxide (N$_2$O) and refrigerant gases such as hydrofluorocarbons (HFCs). Some of these cause more global warming than others. Using CO$_2$e makes it easy to compare the impacts of a range of activities.

Figure 2 shows some estimated examples from *How Bad Are Bananas?* by Mike Berners-Lee.

Travelling one mile...	CO₂e
By pedal bike (powered by bananas)	40 g
By bus (London Routemaster – half-full diesel hybrid)	46 g
By train (intercity – standard class)	80 g
By petrol car (average UK car)	530 g
General	**CO₂e**
A cup of black tea	22 g
A large cows' milk latte	552 g
A toilet roll (virgin paper)	730 g
A paperback book	1 kg
Taking a generous bath (heated by an efficient gas boiler)	1 kg
A pint of cows' milk	1.1 kg
A 10-inch Margherita pizza	1.4 kg
A beef cheeseburger	3.2 kg
A week's food shopping (vegan, no airfreight, no waste)	17 kg
An average week's food shopping (including meat, airfreight)	88 kg
Flying	**CO₂e**
Return flight – London to Hong Kong (economy)	3.5 tons
Return flight – London to Hong Kong (business)	10 tons

FIGURE 2 – CO_2e Examples from *How Bad Are Bananas?*
(Mike Berners-Lee)

To get a sense of your own carbon footprint, visit the World Wide Fund for Nature: footprint.wwf.org.uk.

ALL TALK, NO ACTION?
Are the leaders of your company aware of the important issues related to climate change?

"

Every pound spent is a vote for how we want to live.

"

Mary Portas

1.3. THE PRESSURE'S ON

Against this backdrop, every area of society, government and legislation is under scrutiny. And, increasingly, people are pressing for change.

Naive companies ignore the changing views and behaviour of the people who can affect the very fortunes of their business.

Intelligent companies realize that the very people agitating for change hold the key to a prosperous future. They are an evolving customer base and collectively the company and the consumer can move forward successfully together.

THE NEW CONSCIOUS CONSUMER

Conscious consumers want to purchase goods and services they perceive to be less harmful to the planet and better for society in general. This is on the increase as consumers become more and more aware of the harsh realities associated with many brands and products – such as excessive use of fossil fuels, deforestation, tax avoidance, unacceptable working conditions and modern slavery (see 3.1).

BUSINESS TO BUSINESS

Most companies are part of a supply chain and many contracts now rest on proven sustainability credentials. Failure to provide them often leads to exclusion from the ability to even tender for a contract by responding to an RFP (request for proposal), let alone win it. As you, in turn, look to remove risk from your own supply chain, you will be putting pressure on your suppliers to get their sustainability act together.

EMPLOYEES

More and more employees place deep importance on sustainability – particularly the younger generations (Millennials and Gen Z). The sustainability agenda (including workers' rights, well-being and diversity) affects the recruitment and loyalty of staff, the actions they take and the career decisions they make. Unethical and uncaring companies either lose or fail to attract the best and brightest talent.

INVESTORS

It is no longer acceptable for investors to commit their money to companies with dubious practices. Even ignoring their financial objectives, many are under legislative pressure that forces them to improve standards. Any business currently building to sell will be aware of the pressure to build a robust ESG strategy into its value creation and exit planning. Similarly, those seeking investment should expect deep scrutiny in this area.

Every business is different, as will be the commercial imperatives that support the need for sustainable transformation.

To help establish your company's specific pressure points, try answering the following questions (on a scale of 1-10):

1. How important is ESG to our direct customers (business to consumer or B2C)?
2. How much is ESG now a factor in us winning business to business (B2B) contracts (e.g. requests for proposals – RFPs)?
3. How important is ESG in attracting and retaining good employees?
4. If we need investment, how important will our ESG credentials be in securing this?
5. To what extent is legislation likely to affect our business sector (particularly in view of the government's commitment to Net Zero by 2050)?
6. If we are looking to grow and sell the business, to what extent will ESG be a factor in our value creation (or exit planning)?
7. To what extent is the board leading the ESG agenda (rather than responding to changing external factors)?

Representing these answers in a graph will highlight what's important to your business and help steer decision-making.

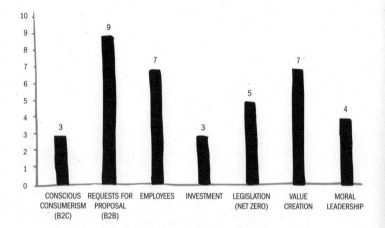

FIGURE 3 – Pressure Points

ALL TALK, NO ACTION?
Are you aware of the strength of feeling of all the stakeholder groups that can influence the fortunes of your business?

"
The transition to net zero is creating the greatest commercial opportunity of our age.

"

Mark Carney, UN Special Envoy on Climate Action and Finance

1.4. THE NEW BUSINESS REALITY

Unless you are an out-and-out climate change denier, or fundamentally disagree with the UK and other governments' commitments to net zero by 2050 (see 2.2), you are probably now recognizing that this situation is serious. If you don't act now, you may no longer have a licence to do business in the foreseeable future. This may be scary in one respect, but it also represents a massive opportunity. Companies that are slow to change have always been the ones left behind, but that doesn't have to be you.

To build resilience and long-term value creation into your business, it pays to think carefully about the important areas shown in *Figure 4*.

COMMERCIAL
Risk mitigation is a big issue. No company can be complacent and assume that its business is secure. Legislation, government commitments and increasing supply chain scrutiny could easily outpace them.

REPUTATIONAL

Reputational risk is real and very tangible. Damage to the business truly can happen overnight in a world that can spot a defect or deception (see 6.2) and publicize it within seconds.

ORGANIZATIONAL

Every organization has its systems, and not all of them are fit for purpose. Legacy approaches are often bad for the planet and bad for the business. Reengineering is frequently needed to ensure long-term sustainability.

MORAL

Sustainable business practices frequently boil down to establishing the right thing to do. Old-style executives in an ivory tower making selfish decisions based on uncontrolled growth and the pursuit of profit at any cost are now exposed. The younger generation have more and more influence on corporate decisions and are making their voices heard.

FIGURE 4 – Areas of Potential Resilience

The size of the prize is significant, so businesses need to change, *for good* (*Figure 5*).

CHANGE	FROM:	TO:
BENEFICIARIES	Shareholders	Multiple stakeholders: employees, customers, suppliers, the planet (see 1.3)
BOTTOM LINE	Single financial bottom line	Triple bottom line: people, planet, profit (see 2.3)
OPERATIONS	Linear: take–make–waste	Circular: closed loop (see 2.4)
MARKET FORCES	Global	Local
GROWTH	Infinite	Green growth, limited growth, degrowth, circular economy (see 2.4)
REPORTING	Short term; quarterly; financial only	Longer term; annual; financial, environmental and social impact reporting (see 6.5)
ADVERTISING	Create consumer demand	Responsible advertising, marketing with integrity (see 6.1)
LEADERSHIP	Heroic, selfish	Transparent, inclusive, nurturing
PRODUCTION	Sourcing the cheapest suppliers possible	Sustainable supply chain management
CONSUMPTION	Hyper-consumerism	Mindful consumption

FIGURE 5 – Change for Good
Adapted from *Sustainable Business: A One Planet Approach*
(Sally Jeanrenaud, Jean-Paul Jeanrenaud and Jonathan Gosling)

ALL TALK, NO ACTION?
Is your company equipped to deal with this new business reality?

1.5. YOU CAN'T MANAGE WHAT YOU DON'T MEASURE

You can have the best of intentions, but unless you establish a proper baseline of what your company does today with clear improvement targets and related actions, you will never make progress towards your sustainability goals.

It is now time to introduce the *PLANET System ESG Audit* to help you begin building a snapshot of where your business stands today on sustainability matters. The audit (also available online at sustainablebusinessbook.com) assesses six areas to provide the foundation for what your *Improvement Plan* will eventually look like (see 3.5).

PLANET SYSTEM *ESG AUDIT*

First, some overview questions:

What does your company do?

Annual turnover:

Number of full-time employees:

Number of business premises:

What is your primary motivation for adopting a more sustainable business approach?

Now answer each of the following questions with Y (Yes), N (No), DK (Don't Know) or N/A (Not Applicable).

If you answer Yes, ask yourself whether you have the relevant data or documentation to prove this point. If so, file it away somewhere safe – most ESG-related accreditation and certification programmes will require written evidence of actions. If not, make a plan to track it properly in the future or establish a written policy or proof of action.

If you answer Don't Know, consider whom to ask to find out.

The remaining answers (No) will form the basic framework for your *Improvement Plan* (see 3.5).

ENVIRONMENTAL IMPACT – SCOPE 1+2[1]

1. Has the company ever calculated its greenhouse gas (GHG) emissions? ☐

    1.1. If yes, were they measured according to a recognized framework (e.g. GHG Protocol, GRI, SASB and TCFD[2])? ☐

    1.2. Was this required under SECR, ESOS, or TCFD[3]? ☐

2. Does the company have Scope 1+2 emissions[1] data from the past two years? ☐

    2.1. If yes, has this data been independently verified/audited (e.g. by a consultancy such as EY or in line with international standard such as ISO 14064[4])? ☐

3. Has the company committed to a specific carbon reduction programme relating to Scope 1+2[1]? ☐

    3.1. If yes, is this aligned with net zero and Science-Based Targets initiative (SBTi)[5]? ☐

    3.2. Or is it aligned with carbon neutrality and PAS 2060[6]? ☐

4. Does the company use a green energy supplier in its business operations? ☐

    4.1. If yes, does this cover gas supplier? ☐

5. Does the company have written energy-efficiency policies? ☐

6. Does the company use energy-efficient lighting systems throughout the operations (e.g. LEDs, sensors)? ☐

7. Does the company use energy-efficient heating and air-conditioning systems throughout its operations? ☐

8. Does the company own any of its own vehicles? If so does it measure the associated emissions? ☐

9. Has the company carbon offset any business activities in the past two years relating to Scope 1+2? ☐

    9.1. If yes, are they independently verified by an internationally recognized organisation (e.g. Gold Standard[7])? ☐

10. Does the company support reforestation, rewilding or biodiversity projects? ☐

ENVIRONMENTAL IMPACT – SCOPE 3[1]

11. Does the company have any Scope 3 emissions[1] data from the past two years? ☐

    11.1. If yes, has this data been independently verified/audited (e.g. by a consultancy such as EY or in line with international standard such as ISO 140644)? ☐

12. Has the company committed to a specific carbon reduction programme relating to Scope 3[1]? ☐

    12.1 If yes, is this aligned with net zero and Science-Based Targets initiative (SBTi)[5]? ☐

    12.2. If carbon neutral and PAS 2060[6] aligned, does it cover your Scope 3 emissions? ☐

13. Does the company have a written water-efficiency policy? ☐

    13.1. Does it use water-efficient systems (e.g. low-flow toilets, showers, water harvesting)? ☐

14. Does the company have clear waste-reduction policies in place? ☐

    14.1. If yes, do they include full written recycling policies? ☐

15. Does the company have a written policy relating to responsible business travel? ☐

    15.1. Are employees incentivized to bike to work? ☐

16. Does the company have specific carbon data or Life Cycle Analysis (LCA) of the products it produces? ☐

17. Does the company have any policies in place regarding product packaging? ☐

18. Does the company have any policies in place regarding low carbon distribution or transportation methods of products? ☐

19. Does the company have a formal, written supplier code of conduct that specifically holds the company's suppliers accountable for social and environmental impact (including basic office supplies and cleaning materials)? ☐

    19.1. Does the company request specific carbon data or Life Cycle Analysis (LCA) of products from suppliers? ☐

20. Has the company carbon offset any business activities in the past two years relating to Scope 3[1]? ☐

20.1. If yes, are they independently verified by an internationally recognized organisation (e.g. Gold Standard[7])? ☐

SOCIAL IMPACT – EMPLOYEES

21. Does the company have an employee handbook? ☐

22. Have employees been surveyed to establish their views and concerns regarding environmental and societal issues? ☐

23. Does the company pay above the 'real' living wage? ☐

24. Does the company have a clear written policy in place covering support for diversity, equality and inclusion? ☐

24.1. Does the company measure or track employee diversity? ☐

24.2. Does the company measure or track board diversity? ☐

25. Has the company recently conducted a pay equity analysis? ☐

26. Does the company hold annual performance reviews? ☐

27. Do all staff have a career and professional development plan? ☐

28. Does the company have an employee health and wellbeing programme? ☐

29. Does the company offer mental health guidance and support? ☐

30. Have employees been supplied with working-from-home guidelines – covering environmental responsibility and physical and mental well-being? ☐

SOCIAL IMPACT – CUSTOMERS

31. Have customers been surveyed to establish their views and concerns regarding environmental and societal issues?

32. Has the company carried out any competitor research around ESG/ sustainability?

33. Are the company's environmental and social credentials clearly and transparently communicated to customers?

34. Does the company clearly communicate responsible care and use of its products to ensure maximum longevity and sustainability?

35. Does the company have any customer initiatives in place to encourage end-of-life product return and/or recycling?

36. Does sustainability play a major part in the company's external marketing and communications strategy?

37. Does the company have checks in place to avoid token corporate environmentalism and greenwashing?

38. Do the company's marketing materials reflect diversity and include under-represented and minority groups?

39. Does the company have official customer feedback and complaints mechanisms?

40. Does the company have official processes in place to monitor customer satisfaction and retention?

SOCIAL IMPACT – COMMUNITY

41. Does the company have a set charitable giving policy? ☐

42. Is a set percentage of company profit or revenue committed to charity on an annual basis? ☐

43. Does the company give away any product or service for free (to those who cannot afford it)? ☐

44. Does the company support local events? ☐

45. Has the company been supporting a local community initiative for over three years? ☐

46. Does the company support employee community service/volunteering? ☐

47. Does the company offer local apprenticeship programmes or internships? ☐

    47.1. Does the company pay apprentices and interns the 'real' living wage? ☐

48. Has the company created any job opportunities for chronically under-employed populations (e.g. at-risk youth, homeless, ex-offenders)? ☐

49. Does the company have specific guidelines in place to work with suppliers who are local, female-owned and/or minority-owned? ☐

50. Does the company bank with an ethical provider? ☐

GOVERNANCE

51. Does ESG play a central role in the company's mission (vision, values and purpose)?

52. Has the company published an ESG or sustainability impact statement or report?

53. Is ESG a fixed agenda item at all board meetings?

54. Does the company have an ESG director, manager, lead or committee?

55. Are environmental and social responsibility criteria built into performance reviews, KPIs (key performance indicators) and bonuses?

56. Is the company currently working with any third party on ESG accreditation?

57. Do the company's central products or services help serve society or preserve the planet in ways that are genuinely aligned with SDGs[8]?

58. Is the company involved in any cross-industry ESG think tanks or United Nations SDG-aligned advocacy projects?

59. Does the company have written policies to cover corporate governance?

    59.1. Do they include whistle-blowing policies?

    59.2. Do they include anti-corruption policies?

    59.3. Do they include anti-bullying policies?

    59.4. Do they include data protection policies?

60. Have all staff received sustainability training including social and environmental responsibility?

1 The GHG Protocol Corporate Standard classifies a company's GHG (greenhouse gas) emissions into three 'scopes.' Scope 1 = direct emissions from owned or controlled sources; Scope 2 = indirect emissions from the generation of purchased energy; Scope 3 = all other indirect emissions that occur in the value or supply chain, including both upstream and downstream emissions (see 2.2).

2 Recognized measurement frameworks include the GHG Protocol, the GRI (Global Reporting Initiative) Standards, the SASB (Sustainability Accounting Standards Board) standards and the TCFD (Task Force on Climate-Related Financial Disclosures) standards.

3 SECR (Streamlined Energy and Carbon Reporting) is required for 'large companies,' which means companies that meet two or more of the following criteria: £36 million or more in turnover, balance sheet assets of £18 million or more, and 250 or more employees. The ESOS (Energy Savings Opportunity Scheme) is for 'large undertakings,' which are classified as those with 250 or more employees, a turnover in excess of £44 million and an annual balance sheet in excess of £38 million. Compliance with the TCFD (Task Force on Climate-Related Financial Disclosures) is now mandatory for 'large companies' in the UK, which are those with 500 or more employees and a turnover of more than £500 million. Check the current criteria for the latest information.

4 ISO 14064 is the international standard that serves as a guideline for following the GHG Protocol.

5 Net zero strategies should be aligned with the Science Based Targets initiative (SBTi), which in turn is aligned with the 1.5°c pathway (see 2.1). Currently this means halving emissions by 2030, and by 2050 being close to zero emissions, with only unavoidable residual emissions being neutralized (offset).

6 Carbon neutrality strategies are often aligned with PAS 2060 – a less stringent specification standard that details how to demonstrate carbon neutrality through measurement, reduction and offsetting. PAS 2060 is produced and published by the British Standards Institution (BSI).

7 Gold Standard, more accurately known as Gold Standard for the Global Goals, is an industry-leading certification standard that is used to verify carbon offset projects.

8 The United Nations Sustainable Development Goals (SDGs) were adopted by all member nations in 2015. The 17 SDGs recognize that "ending poverty and other deprivations must go hand in hand with strategies that improve health and education, reduce inequality, and spur economic growth – all while tackling climate change and working to preserve our oceans and forests" (see 2.1).

For more definitions, see the A–Z of Helpful Terms.

ALL TALK, NO ACTION?
Have you completed the PLANET System ESG Audit?

IS THE BOARD ON BOARD?

It is time to confront the issues directly by:

- *Acknowledging that this is a serious problem*
- *Cutting out talking shops and concentrating on fast decision-making*
- *Flushing out secret sceptics and getting the issues out into the open*
- *Exposing artificial harmony and having proper, robust discussions*
- *Overcoming inertia by establishing accountability*
- *Completing the PLANET System ESG Audit*

TO DO LIST

STEP TWO – LEARN
GET PROPERLY
INFORMED

The L of the PLANET System stands for **LEARN**.

A company that already knows the severity of the situation can begin looking at the gaps in its knowledge.

What do you need to **LEARN** about and understand before you formulate a plan?

This is inevitably quite a technical part of the book, but it only takes 15 minutes to read. All the terms are explained in the *A–Z of Helpful Terms* at the back of the book.

This stage is predominantly educational, informing you about all the important issues relating to sustainability in a rapid, easily decipherable way.

STEP TWO
LEARN

2.1. BOUNDARIES, SDGS AND COP

In hindsight, it seems obvious that the unprecedented population boom and associated socio-economic trends of the Great Acceleration (see 1.1) would place enormous strain on our planet's resources. And that's exactly what Johan Rockstrom and a group of internationally renowned scientists identified in 2009. They came up with a set of planetary boundaries – nine environmental parameters within which humanity can develop and thrive for generations to come, so long as they are not exceeded. These planetary boundaries are: 1. climate change, 2. ocean acidification, 3. chemical pollution, 4. fertilizer use, 5. freshwater withdrawals, 6. land conversion, 7. biodiversity loss, 8. air pollution and 9. ozone layer depletion.

In an Oxfam discussion paper of 2012 called *A Safe and Just Space for Humanity*, Kate Raworth combined the concept of these planetary boundaries with a complementary concept of social boundaries – 1. food, 2. health, 3. education, 4. income and work, 5. peace and justice, 6. political voice, 7. social equity, 8. gender equality, 9. housing, 10. energy and 11. water – bringing them into a single framework as shown in *Figure 6*.

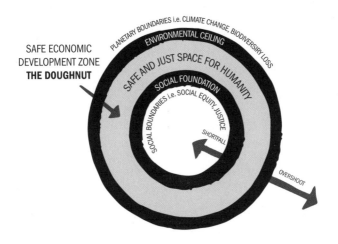

SAFE ECONOMIC
DEVELOPMENT ZONE
THE DOUGHNUT

PLANETARY BOUNDARIES i.e. CLIMATE CHANGE, BIODIVERSIRY LOSS

ENVIRONMENTAL CEILING

SAFE AND JUST SPACE FOR HUMANITY

SOCIAL FOUNDATION

SOCIAL BOUNDARIES i.e. SOCIAL EQUITY, JUSTICE

SHORTFALL

OVERSHOOT

FIGURE 6 – Doughnut Economics

In this framework, the social foundation forms the inner circle
and the environmental ceiling forms an outer boundary. Between
the two boundaries lies an area – shaped like a doughnut – that
represents an environmentally safe and socially just space
in which humanity can thrive. It is also the space in which
sustainable economic development can take place – hence the
term *doughnut economics*.

It's sad to report that at the time of writing, we are overshooting
the environmental ceiling in a number of areas including –
crucially – biodiversity loss and climate change. Plus, we are
seeing shortfalls in many of our fundamental social foundations,
such as political voice, peace and justice, and social equity.

For long-term stability and sustainability, we need to bring these back into the safe economic development zone: the doughnut.

In 2015, our global governments showed their understanding of this complex interrelationship between the planet and society through the adoption of the United Nations 2030 Agenda for Sustainable Development – a shared blueprint for peace and prosperity for people and the planet, now and into the future. At its heart are the 17 *Sustainable Development Goals* (SDGs), which are an urgent call for action by all countries.

The 17 SDGs (*Figure* 7) recognize that ending poverty and other deprivations must go hand in hand with strategies that improve health and education, reduce inequality and spur economic growth – all while tackling climate change and working to preserve our oceans and forests.

FIGURE 7 – The Sustainable Development Goals (SDGs)

The Paris Agreement in 2015 (COP 21) also saw the introduction of NDCs – *nationally determined contributions*. These embody efforts or commitments by each country to reduce its national emissions and adapt to the impacts of climate change.

Fast forward to 2021 and COP 26 in Glasgow. Many would say that major progress on these commitments was stifled because of Covid-19. However, the primary message to come out of COP 26 was to "Keep 1.5°C Alive."

1.5°C is the maximum increase in global temperature that scientists agree is needed to avoid catastrophic consequences for people and our living environment. To achieve this, the world needs to reach *net zero* by 2050.

ALL TALK, NO ACTION?
Is your team thoroughly familiar with the SDGs and their implications?

2.2. DECIPHERING NET ZERO

Countries and companies worldwide are now talking about net zero and, on paper at least, an ever-growing percentage of our global economy is committed to achieving this by 2050. The UK made a legally binding commitment in 2019 to reach net zero by this date.

Net zero transition plans need to be consistent with a global temperature rise of no more than 1.5°C above pre-industrial levels. It's a complex area but, massively simplified, what this means is that businesses need to:

Step One: Establish their baseline carbon emissions *now*.
Step Two: Reduce them by at least 50% by 2030.
Step Three: Reach net zero emissions (or at least reduce them by 90%) before 2050.

The Net Zero Standard, from the *Science-Based Targets initiative* (SBTi), was launched in October 2021 and provides the most robust framework for businesses aiming to set net zero targets aligned with science. It requires an organization to consider its greenhouse gas (GHG) emissions throughout its operations, including its supply chain.

This is in line with the *GHG Protocol Corporate Standard*, which classifies a company's GHG emissions into three 'scopes' (*Figure 8*):

Scope 1: Direct emissions from owned or controlled sources (e.g. gas for heating and/or cooking, and fuel used in company-owned vehicles).
Scope 2: Indirect emissions from the generation of purchased energy (e.g. purchased electricity).
Scope 3: All other indirect emissions that occur in the value or supply chain, including both *upstream* and *downstream* emissions.

Upstream emissions: those that occur during the life cycle of a material or product up to the point of sale by the producer (including all the raw materials, transportation of those materials to assembly or manufacturing, and business travel).

Downstream emissions: those that occur during the life cycle of a material or product after its sale by the producer (including distribution and storage, use of the product and end of life).

See also Life Cycle Analysis (LCA) - 2.4.

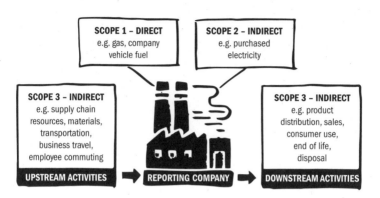

FIGURE 8 – Emissions: Scopes 1, 2 + 3 (Upstream and Downstream)

At the time of publication, the SBTi's certification criteria for net zero require the following commitments:

Near term: 95% Scope 1+2 reduction and 67% Scope 3 reduction by 2030.
Long term: 95% Scope 1+2 reduction and 90% Scope 3 reduction by 2050.

NOTE: There are other decarbonizing terms and frameworks – for example carbon neutrality which is aligned with the British Standards Institution's PAS 2060. This differs from net zero in several ways. It does not require any specific ambition (such as the 1.5°C pathway). It also does not require Scope 3 emissions to be included, although this is encouraged. It can be product specific rather than companywide. And, although carbon reduction plans are encouraged, an organization can jump straight to neutralizing emissions through purchasing high-quality offsets and still claim carbon neutrality.

A WORD ON CARBON OFFSETTING

This is another highly complex area. However, in short, there will inevitably always be emissions that cannot be reduced any further. So, to reach net zero, these unavoidable emissions need to be compensated for (through offsetting) or neutralized (through removal programmes).

For example, for every ton of unavoidable CO_2e produced by a company's business operations, the company can fund offset projects to reduce the amount of CO_2e in the atmosphere. Common carbon reduction projects include protecting forests, developing clean energy sources and introducing more efficient energy products.

A word of caution, though. From a commercial perspective, if a company relies heavily on proceeding straight to purchasing offsets without a robust reduction strategy, the amount that it pays on an annual basis will inevitably keep going up. From an environmental standpoint, offsetting can be viewed as mopping up the floor without turning the tap off. Neither is good.

To ensure that you are offsetting with integrity, always consider the points mentioned in *Figure 9*.

Good carbon offsets must always be...

1. **Real:** Has the emissions reduction actually happened? In practice this means carbon credits are only issued *after* the emissions reduction has taken place – not on the 'promise' of a future emissions reduction.
2. **Measurable:** All emissions reductions must be quantifiable using recognized measurement tools, against a credible baseline.
3. **Permanent:** In practice this means that carbon credits must represent emissions reductions for at least 100 years.
4. **Additional:** Can the project demonstrate that the reduction in emissions could not have occurred if it weren't for carbon finance?
5. **Independently verified:** Emissions reductions should be verified by an independent third party that is approved by one of the international standards.
6. **Unique:** No more than one carbon credit can be associated with one ton of CO_2 reduced. Carbon credits are stored and recorded on an independent registry, which ensures no double counting.

FIGURE 9 – Carbon Offsetting with Integrity

ALL TALK, NO ACTION?

Have you established your company's baseline carbon emissions?

2.3. PEOPLE, PLANET, PROFIT

Many businesses still see sustainability as a necessary evil – something they must now do whether they like it or not. Others, however, are seeing this as an opportunity to change the way they view success, redressing the bias towards the relentless pursuit of profit with little regard for the health of people and the planet.

Rather than focusing on the traditional bottom line, responsible businesses are adopting the *triple bottom line* – people, planet *and* profit (*Figure 10*). This term was coined by sustainability pioneer John Elkington. It describes a business model that forces companies to focus not just on profits but also on high business integrity and environmental sensitivity – resulting in both successful business strategy *and* moral business practices.

FIGURE 10 – The Triple Bottom Line

It should be noted that in his 2020 book *Green Swans*, Elkington talks of retracting the concept of the triple bottom line – not because it is bad, but because he is dismayed by how it is being used (or misused) in many businesses today.

He feels that many organizations are hiding behind the construct, just paying lip service to it and using it as a tick-box exercise, without any genuine desire to change the fundamentals of their commercially driven business models.

Like so much surrounding sustainability, to create real change with integrity, it is important to embark on this journey with genuine commitment, not just for PR purposes.

> Profit is not in itself a bad thing – businesses need to be commercially viable. It's how you make the profit and what you do with it that matter.

It takes time and effort to embed this thinking into a business. Financial reporting has internationally recognized frameworks. Non-financial reporting is less established and therefore less clearly and consistently measured.

ALL TALK, NO ACTION?
Are you genuinely prepared to balance the triple bottom line of people, planet and profit?

2.4. GOING CIRCULAR

At the heart of a lot of sustainability thinking is the recognition that we need to embrace a more circular way of thinking.

The *circular economy model* is inspired by natural living systems and promotes the fact that there is no such thing as waste in nature.

Unlike the traditional linear approach of take–make–use–waste, a circular economy is a sustainable closed-loop model (*Figure 11*).

It creates value through product recapture and then recycling, restoring and reusing product elements in remanufacturing – thereby radically limiting the extraction of raw materials at the beginning of a product's life and the production of waste at the end.

In essence, it involves keeping products and materials in use for as long as possible. The concept is driving new trends in repurposing items, easy home repair and second-hand purchasing.

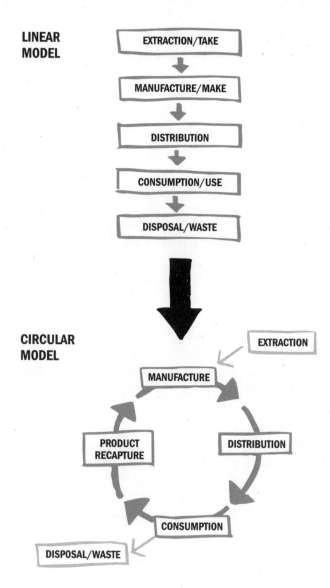

FIGURE 11 – From Linear to Circular

The circular economy concept also challenges the necessity of owning products in the way that we are traditionally used to doing. It is access to what the product provides that is important, rather than the product itself. Understanding this shift in mindset lays the groundwork for shifting our economy from linear to circular and can be seen in many examples today, from car-sharing clubs to fashion rental.

Intelligent modern businesses are asking whether their customers can rent or lease their products instead of buying them outright – with the business keeping the same level of income or profit. This moves away from the *built-in obsolescence* seen often in products today (particularly tech), which is designed to encourage regular new purchases rather than lifetime use.

Other interconnected concepts include biomimicry, natural capitalism, cradle to cradle, frugal innovation and the inertia principle – all outlined in the *A–Z of Helpful Terms*.

LIFE CYCLE ANALYSIS (LCA)

A Life Cycle Analysis (LCA) is a way of calculating the overall impact that a certain product has on the environment throughout its life. This is often highly complex, as there are many steps in producing even the simplest items. Starting with the extraction of raw materials like metals and rock from the ground, chemicals from plants, wood from trees, and glass from sand. These raw materials then need to be transported to a place where they are made (or manufactured) into parts and put together to create the final product.

When the product is made, it needs to be distributed for sale (either directly to the customer or via a wholesaler or third party). Additional resources may be needed to repair or return items. And ultimately, to dispose of it when it is no longer working or needed (its end of life).

All these stages have an impact on the environment, and all of them use energy. To properly understand the impact of your product, a Life Cycle Analysis will help you plot every step.

ALL TALK, NO ACTION?

Have you considered all the various ways you can introduce circular thinking into your business?

"

He who has a 'why' can bear any 'how'.

Friedrich Nietzsche

2.5. BUSINESS AS A FORCE FOR GOOD

There is much talk about purpose in business these days, but what does it mean? In short, your purpose should be greater than the products you make or the services you provide.

In his book *The Infinite Game*, Simon Sinek refers to a company's "just cause" as the thing that gives purpose to organizations. If you're working on something bigger than any particular short-term win, then your days take on meaning and feel more fulfilling. However, Sinek warns that if the words of a just cause are used simply to boost a brand image, attract employees or help drive a short-term goal, then the impact will be short-lived.

At the heart of establishing a wider moral purpose is the recognition that *doing good and making money are not incompatible*. But this should not be forced. For this to be genuine and become part of the true culture of the business, it is essential to include employees. This will ensure future buy-in and guard against dilution, or fizzle-out, as your purpose permeates through your business (see 4.5). Also involve customers and other relevant stakeholders. Find out what is important to them (see 3.1). Most crucially, remember that *purpose without performance is simply PR*.

Certified B Corporation

If you really want to place purpose and sustainability at the heart of your business and become a force for good, you may wish to consider becoming a Certified B Corporation – something that the authors achieved in 2022. This is a movement of businesses that meet the highest standards of verified social and environmental performance, public transparency and legal accountability to balance profit and purpose. To view the process for your business, see assessment criteria, and download guides and checklists, visit bcorporation.net.

The Better Business Act is a campaign initiated by B Lab (the non-profit organization behind B Corp Certification) and supported by

over 1,000 UK businesses. This coalition is pushing for an amendment to the Companies Act to ensure that the purpose of business includes an official commitment to benefiting wider society and the environment, in addition to shareholders' pockets. To join the coalition for a "cleaner, greener, fairer future for all," visit betterbusinessact.org.

There are many other options for verifying your sustainable business credentials, many of which will be industry specific. For some examples, see the list of websites at the end of the *References, Resources and Further Reading* section.

ACTIONS SPEAK LOUDER THAN WORDS

To really put your money where your mouth is, you may wish to consider non-paying customers in your business model. This is what Larry Weber refers to in his book *Authentic Marketing* as "paying it forward." He recommends asking the following big questions:

Who in the world would most benefit if they had access to our product or service?

How can we set up a programme to provide access to our products or services to those people in need?

Once you have identified people who would benefit most from your product or service but are unable to afford it, you can develop a plan to incorporate an element of free distribution into your business model. Reinventing the old promotional tool of buy one, get one free as *buy one, GIVE one free* is a fantastic example of paying it forward and has been used by a number of innovative, thoughtful businesses, such as Mindful Chef and Hey Girls.

Of course, not all organizations can commit to the full buy one, give one model. If this wouldn't work for your business, consider instead a *buy one, give SOMETHING* approach. Existing initiatives to look out for here include 1% for the Planet and Pledge 1%. Both promote committing a minimum percentage of your company's revenue – or sometimes profit, equity or employee time – to your chosen charitable causes.

ALL TALK, NO ACTION?

Does everyone in your company agree that doing good and making money are not incompatible, or are there disagreements and tensions?

IS THE BOARD ON BOARD?

It is time to get properly informed by:

- *Admitting what you don't know and finding out more*
- *Establishing what important decision-makers have truly learned*
- *Clarifying which critical people have discussed and accepted the new information*
- *Challenging the linear nature of your business*
- *Becoming comfortable with technical information so as to avoid superficial conversations*

TO DO LIST

STAGE 2

STRATEGY

STEP THREE – AGREE
DECIDE YOUR
STRATEGIC DIRECTION

The A of the PLANET System stands for **AGREE**.

This is one of the hardest parts: getting everyone to agree with each other.

Companies are riddled with disagreement, stemming from rifts in boards, those who are resistant to change and those who keep worrying about money while ignoring what is the right thing to do.

Few meetings end with a unanimous decision. So it is crucial that a strategic direction is clearly decided upon, without any room for misunderstanding, and that everyone signs up to it.

This stage uses the *PLANET System ESG Audit* as a basis for designing and agreeing an *Improvement Plan*.

STEP THREE

AGREE

3.1. FIFTY SHADES OF GREEN

We looked at the *new business reality* at the beginning of the book (see 1.4). Now that you have understood the implications of that, it is time to break it down into manageable parts to help you move to agreement and, ultimately, action.

It is very difficult to get people to agree without first working out what the specific driving factors are for your business. The best way to establish that is to ask all the people involved. That is why the most important component of the **AGREE** step is conducting surveys to establish the true motivations of everyone involved.

For many, this is a mental struggle between the heart and the head. You might feel that something is the right thing to do, but your head gets dragged back into the grim working reality of just, well, making money. Often this conflict is disguised, denied or not even discussed. While that may create a form of artificial harmony at the beginning of the process, it will be a false dawn because in truth there is no agreement – merely the absence of disagreement. Strong resistance is likely to follow later – either overtly or simply through inertia – and it could well scupper the whole thing.

To establish strength of feeling and underlying motivation, these types of interested parties need to be asked for their views:

- The board or senior leadership team
- Employees
- Customers
- Supply partners
- Investors

When dealing with customers, it is important at this stage to understand the difference between a business that deals with other businesses (B2B) and one that sells products and services directly to consumers (B2C), because their motivations can be very different. The rising numbers of more *conscious consumers* come in a range of shades. So-called *light green* consumers want to satisfy their moral conscience on ethical matters with just enough reassurance about the sustainability credentials of a product, service or brand. They can be relatively easy to assuage with broad claims that products are 'eco', 'green', 'natural', 'environmentally friendly' and so on, but beware greenwashing (see 6.2). So-called *dark green* consumers are more likely to be activists and boycotters of products. It is crucial to understand just how green your audience is (see *Figure 12*).

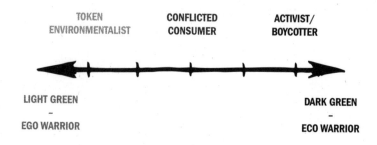

FIGURE 12 – Shades of Green Consumerism

B2B company approaches are likely to be process and procedure based (e.g. managed via procurement) and therefore subject to deep scrutiny. Tenders and contracts are won and lost on highly specific sustainability criteria, and the old trick of hiding deficiencies further down the supply chain no longer washes with eagle-eyed procurement departments. In many cases now, without credible sustainability credentials, a company may not even be able to tender for business, let alone win it.

Survey data will provide one level of information. Workshops can provide much more detail and are likely to bring contrasting views to the surface faster, along with initial ideas for possible remedies and solutions.

ALL TALK, NO ACTION?
Have you designed and sent out surveys to all relevant parties?

"

We cannot solve our problems with the same thinking we used when we created them.

"

Albert Einstein

3.2. CHALLENGE THE STATUS QUO

In other words, old thinking won't solve new problems and running your business as you always have done is no longer sustainable.

Starting a modern business from scratch makes it proportionally easier to design every part of the process in a sustainable way, but this is much harder for older, established businesses. In almost every case, the manufacturing process and the way these older companies are organized were not set up with *people* and the *planet* in mind – just profit. Many have tried to retrofit sustainable thinking into the business, but it's not easy, and many fail.

Part of this failure can simply be down to entrenched executives still being trapped in old ways of thinking. Their attitude of "We've always done it that way" prevents forward motion. That is why it is imperative to challenge the status quo. Everything must be confronted and rethought. In his book *Eating the Big Fish*, Adam Morgan urges those running companies to break with their immediate past – forget everything you know and think again.

Intelligent ways to change the company for the better will once again come from surveys and workshops. In times gone by, answers to the question "What does success look like?" tended to gravitate towards money-related issues such as growth, revenue and EBITDA (earnings before interest, tax, depreciation and amortization). This relentless concentration on cash is no longer enough (see 2.3). Companies need a new set of sustainability metrics that challenge everything, including areas such as employee satisfaction, charity contribution, staff churn levels and mental health, and carbon reduction progress (see 1.5). These are all new things to nurture and value as part of a drive towards good growth.

The old way is a scenario in which the owner or investor is in the predominant role, exploiting resources (including people) for money. For this idea, many blame the economist Milton Friedman, who in the 1970s asserted that the purpose of a company is to make money for shareholders. The new way needs to adhere to new rules for sustainable growth.

"

Is the world a better place because your business is in it?

"

Net Positive,
Paul Polman and Andrew Winston

Someone once said that it's hard to be green when you are in the red, so the profit element remains important, but *not at the expense of people and the planet*. Good growth comes through engaging motivated talent, investing appropriately in improving operations, following the science and adapting to change for good (see 1.4).

THE POWER OF DIVERSITY

Another point to consider when challenging the status quo is the value of diverse thinking. This is needed to provide breadth, and commitment must come from all over the company. You will need the views of all ages, levels, skills and backgrounds to solve the hardest of problems. You may also need the help of those outside the company, such as suppliers, customers and even competitors. Use every resource you have to solve problems and plan, and be sure to engage as many people as possible in the whole process. This will increase the chances of you being able to break seemingly insurmountable problems down into manageable steps, identify the barriers and overcome any resistance (see 4.3). By definition, the more people involved, the fewer the obstacles.

Embracing diversity of contribution leads to diverse thinking, which is always stronger and more effective. In her book *Diversify*, June Sarpong highlights how our general fear of the 'other' (whatever 'other' is for you) subconsciously influences our behaviour. She proposes six types of integration, as shown in *Figure 13*.

- **Challenge your ism:** Beware of your conscious and unconscious bias
- **Check your circle:** Don't just talk to the people you usually do
- **Connect with the others:** Seek out people you wouldn't normally
- **Change your mind:** Be prepared to accept another view
- **Celebrate difference:** Find the best that alternative views can offer
- **Champion the cause:** There is more power in unity than division

FIGURE 13 – Integrating Diverse Thinking

Challenging the status quo and encouraging broader thinking lead to smarter solutions.

ALL TALK, NO ACTION?
Have you solicited a wide range of opinions in order to challenge the status quo?

3.3. AN INSIDE JOB?

Many companies make the fatal mistake of viewing sustainability as a 'project,' sitting outside the traditional core business structure (*Figure 14*).

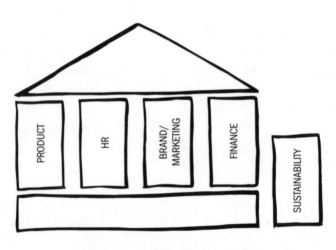

FIGURE 14 – Sustainability as a Project

Or they place sustainability within an existing discipline, often HR or marketing (*Figure 15*).

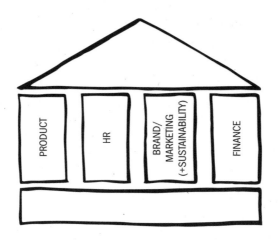

FIGURE 15 – Sustainability Falling within an Existing Department or Discipline

But, in reality, it's a complete change in attitude that must permeate the entire operation from top to bottom (*Figure 16*).

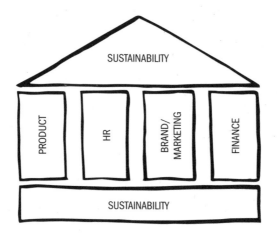

FIGURE 16 – Sustainability Permeating the Entire Operation

This philosophy of *sustainability is not a project* has a deep bearing on the organizational structure of a company. It is essential that sustainability becomes part of a company's culture, providing the bedrock of all its activities or an overarching filter for all decision-making. It is also vital that proper resource is dedicated to it, even if the company starts modestly by engaging an external consultant and then builds its internal capacity to handle sustainability full time.

If the sustainability function stands alone, or is hidden away within another department, then it will be doomed to failure. There are scores of examples of where this unenlightened approach has left anyone representing the function without any executive authority to enact the change that is needed.

So, don't ***do*** sustainability, ***be*** sustainable.

ALL TALK, NO ACTION?
Is the sustainability function in your company viewed as a separate department?

3.4. EVERYONE, EVERYWHERE

Sustainable thinking needs to permeate all aspects of a business and be thoroughly understood by all employees. Whether you have five or 5,000 people, if you change their behaviour (including your own), then you have changed the company.

To be clear, this is not a case of deviously handing the responsibility for the world's problems from the company to the individual in the same way that many argue that fossil fuel companies invented personal carbon calculators to make it look as though individuals were responsible for emissions rather than them.

Instead, collective responsibility means making sure that people routinely stop, think and challenge all business decisions (*Figure 17*).

STOP, THINK, CHALLENGE.

- Is there a greener way of doing this?
- Is there a kinder way of doing this?
- Is there a more inclusive way of doing this?
- Is there a more thoughtful way of doing this?

FIGURE 17 – Stop, Think, Challenge

An entire cultural shift is needed to make sure that everything is consistently questioned through a sustainability lens.

For example, if everyone in an organization instinctively challenges their purchasing on behalf of the company (and indeed at home), significant change can occur. One way to do this is to use a responsible purchasing checklist (see *Figure 18*).

Responsible purchasing checklist	
Do we really need this?	
What is it made of?	
What is it wrapped in?	
Where is it coming from?	
Who made it?	
How will it be transported and delivered?	
Is it built to last?	
How will it be disposed of (where will it end up)?	
Is there a greener, more responsible option?	

FIGURE 18 – Responsible Purchasing Checklist

This approach does, however, come with a small health warning. It is the responsibility of those taking any action to consider the likely consequences of that action, some of which can be unforeseen. Every action has a reaction. There will inevitably be tensions when balancing corporate impacts on people versus the planet. Eventually, something has to give. Jumping to solutions can lead to unwanted or unforeseen consequences. Here's a simple example. In good faith, a company decides to reduce the impact of buying materials in its supply chain from a developing country overseas, thereby lowering its carbon emissions and transportation costs. As a result of this, people in that underdeveloped community are deprived of the income that they had, so there is an unfortunate knock-on effect on their livelihoods.

So, doing the right thing when it comes to sustainability is not always as simple as you might think. In almost every business category, the issue has many moving parts. There is often built-in complexity and decisions are rarely binary. Instead of having a nice, simple choice between A and B, you will usually face a chain reaction that needs to be scrutinized and anticipated.

Many businesses have felt they were on the right track only to be confronted by the unexpected – Donald Rumsfeld's notorious *unknown unknowns*. Pandemic, war, shortage of parts and inflation are all 'unexpected' and are often used as an excuse or distraction to deviate from long-term sustainability goals. It is tempting to put out short-term fires under the heading of a crisis or business survival and use these as excuses to delay sustainability initiatives. But it is detrimental in the long run, because all you are doing is ignoring the *chronic* in favour of the *acute*.

ALL TALK, NO ACTION?
Does everyone in the organization make decisions through a sustainability lens?

3.5. PROVE IT AND IMPROVE IT

Reaching agreement is easier said than done. And so is getting it done. Agreeing to agree takes tremendous effort, and it is so easy to fall into the perennial trap of all talk and no action, or mainly talk and just a bit of action. This in turn often leads to greenwashing (see 6.2), because the truth behind the external claim is actually much more flimsy than it sounds.

So, to conclude this step, it is really important to agree a framework to demonstrate the progress of your improvement.

The first task here is to review the findings of your *PLANET System ESG Audit* (1.5). Your reactions and answers to the various questions and subject areas will push you on to an *Improvement Plan*. This should be built step by step, as in *Figure 19*:

- If you have answered Yes to a particular question in the Audit, that's great. Now make sure you can prove it, with established and verified data, and then diligently file it. This will stand you in good stead if or when you decide to go for some form of certification or accreditation.

- At this point it is also worth deciding (agreeing) whether this activity or initiative is something you want to share with your employees, customers and suppliers as part of your overall sustainability communication plan or *Impact Report*. If Yes, keep it safe – we will revisit this in Stage 6: TELL (see 6.5).

- If you have answered No to a particular question and agree that it is unfeasible, unrealistic or not applicable to your business, then ignore it for now.

- If you have answered No to a particular question and agree that it is something you want to commit to achieving in the future, this should become an action item in your *Improvement Plan*.

For a full working version of this, see sustainablebusinessbook.com.

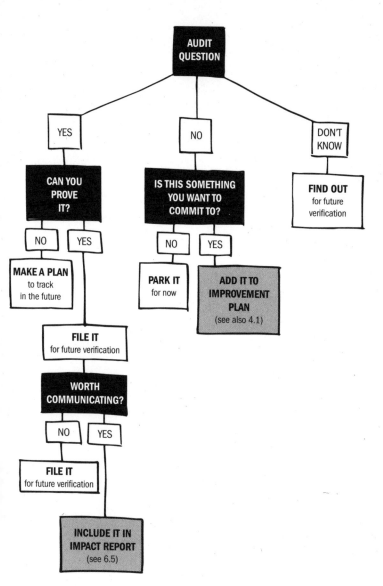

FIGURE 19 – _PLANET System ESG Audit_ Flow Chart

Once you have worked through all the operational areas in your business, you will most likely have created a long list of areas for improvement – *Figure 20* gives a few examples.

BASIC IMPROVEMENT PLAN EXAMPLE

ENVIRONMENTAL – SCOPE 1+2

Commit to a net zero (SBTi aligned) carbon reduction programme relating to Scope 1+2

Switch to a green energy supplier in all business operations

ENVIRONMENTAL – SCOPE 3

Establish a plan to start calculating Scope 3 emissions data

Establish a written water efficiency policy

SOCIAL IMPACT – EMPLOYEES

Conduct a pay equity analysis

Survey employees to establish their views and concerns regarding environmental and societal issues

SOCIAL IMPACT – CUSTOMERS

Carry out competitor research on ESG/sustainability

Review how environmental and social initiatives and credentials are communicated to customers

SOCIAL IMPACT – COMMUNITY

Agree a minimum percentage of profit or revenue to commit to charity on an annual basis

Establish a programme to support local apprenticeships

GOVERNANCE

Review organization's mission (vision, values and purpose) and ensure ESG plays a central role

Include ESG as fixed item at all board or senior leadership meetings

FIGURE 20 – Basic *Improvement Plan*

This is the foundation for your *Improvement Plan*. You have agreed in principle what needs to be done and you can now move on to creating a more detailed framework to help you manage and prioritize initiatives. We will guide you through this in the next stage (see 4.1).

ALL TALK, NO ACTION?
Have you constructed your Improvement Plan?

IS THE BOARD ON BOARD?

It is time to decide your strategic direction by:

- *Establishing and agreeing what is driving your sustainable approach*
- *Challenging the status quo vigorously*
- *Planning for the unexpected*
- *Embedding sustainability into the entire company*
- *Creating the basis of your Improvement Plan*

TO DO LIST

STEP FOUR – NAVIGATE
OVERCOME OBSTACLES

The N of the PLANET System stands for **NAVIGATE**.

It is important to work out what all the obstacles to change are. All companies have them, whether they are organizational, budgetary, structural, or simply from individuals not agreeing or refusing to change their behaviour.

The ability to **NAVIGATE** through all this requires intelligent planning and honesty from all decision-makers.

This stage takes your *Improvement Plan* as a foundation and breaks it down into more detail so that everyone knows precisely what they need to do and by when.

STEP FOUR
NAVIGATE

4.1. EAT THE ELEPHANT

Many of you will have heard the old joke: how do you eat an elephant? The answer is: one mouthful at a time. Not hilarious, perhaps, but it makes an interesting point about how building a resilient modern business is never going to be an easy task. And it's even harder reengineering an old one to make it fit for the future.

The PLANET System requires soul-searching and data-mining. By this point, you may have a long and possibly overwhelming list of things to do. Viewed as a whole, it can often feel so enormous that it is hard or downright impossible to see an intelligent way through. So the next step is to break your *Improvement Plan* down into manageable chunks.

Follow these steps using *Figure 21*:

A. Decide which **Business Area** the action or initiative falls under.

B. Establish whether this is a **Quick Win** or whether it is **Strategic** and therefore longer term. An additional helpful tool here is the *Minimum Effort, Maximum Impact* framework (see *Figure 22*).

C. Is this initiative aligned with a particular **Sustainable Development Goal** (see 2.1)?

D. Put a **Timeframe** on it, such as:
    - 6 months
    - 24 months
    - By 2030
    - By 2050

E. Put a realistic **Financial or Human Resource Implication** against each action item.

F. Mark one **Person Ultimately Responsible** for each action item. If more than one person is specified, the action item is unlikely to happen because each will wait for the other to act.

G. Establish some **Measurement Criteria** to ensure you know when the action will be deemed to have been achieved.

H. Start noting **Potential Barriers** (see 4.2).

I. Add a final line to note when the action has been **Completed**. Once it has been achieved, make sure you have the right data to verify it, and file this for potential future certification or accreditation. Then decide whether you want it to be part of your overall sustainability communications plan or *Impact Report* (see 6.5).

	A	B	C	D
EXPANDED IMPROVEMENT PLAN	Business Area	Quick Win or Strategic (see Minimum Effort, Maximum Impact)	SDG Alignment	Target Timeframe
ENVIRONMENTAL – SCOPE 1+2				
Add initiatives				
ENVIRONMENTAL – SCOPE 3				
Add initiatives				
SOCIAL IMPACT – EMPLOYEES				
Add initiatives				
SOCIAL IMPACT – CUSTOMERS				
Add initiatives				
SOCIAL IMPACT – COMMUNITY				
Add initiatives				
GOVERNANCE				
Add initiatives				

FIGURE 21 – Expanded *Improvement Plan*

E	F	G	H	I
Financial or Human Resource Implication	Person Ultimately Responsible	Measurement Criteria. What does success look like?	Potential Barriers (see Identifying Barriers framework)	Completed Y/N?

Download the full *Improvement Plan* template at sustainablebusinessbook.com.

MINIMUM EFFORT, MAXIMUM IMPACT

A straightforward way to establish the effort needed to get these tasks done versus the impact they will have on the business, is to use the Minimum Effort, Maximum Impact grid (*Figure 22*). This makes it easy to identify early quick wins that require minimum effort but will deliver maximum impact.

HIGH IMPACT/LOW EFFORT   HIGH IMPACT/HIGH EFFORT

QUICK WIN   STRATEGIC

HOUSEKEEPING   RETHINK

LOW IMPACT/LOW EFFORT   LOW IMPACT/HIGH EFFORT

FIGURE 22 – Minimum Effort, Maximum Impact
Adapted from *Conscious Capitalism Field Guide*
(Raj Sisodia, Timothy Henry and Thomas Eckschmidt)

ALL TALK, NO ACTION?
Have you broken the plan down into bite-sized chunks?

4.2. IDENTIFY BARRIERS

Sustainability is a never-ending journey. You can't navigate unless you know what's in the way. That's why you need a decent and accurate map. Maps tell you what lies ahead, what you need to go round, what you need to climb over and whether you need to change your method of getting to where you're trying to go.

Moving the business towards a more responsible and resilient future requires a large dose of pragmatism. You have to be realistic. In the same way that all talk, no action leaves a company stranded in an idealistic dreamland where nothing is actually happening, it is essential to identify the barriers that are standing in your way (*Figure 23*).

Here are seven types of barrier that might afflict an organization:

- **Institutional:** What you do and the way you do it
- **Logistical:** How you move goods and people around
- **Structural:** The state of your buildings and physical assets
- **Financial:** How you budget and pay for everything
- **Departmental:** How you are organized and the degree to which you operate in silos
- **Practical:** Your day-to-day activities and how effectively your teams work
- **Attitudinal:** Whether individuals or entire departments want to change things for the better

FIGURE 23 – Identifying Barriers

These are a few examples of what happens in many companies, but there are probably many more. Use this extension to the *Improvement Plan* to map out the barriers that are likely to cause the most impediment to your intentions (*Figure 24*), and then you can move on to working out how to overcome them. Although at first glance this may seem like a somewhat depressing or pessimistic approach, it reaps tremendous benefits because once the full extent of the likely resistance is known, you have a much better chance of navigating through it or breaking the barriers down entirely. With the right attitude and approach, there is always a way through.

BUSINESS AREA	INITIATIVE	POTENTIAL BARRIERS	TYPE(S): · Institutional · Logistical · Structural · Financial · Departmental · Practical · Attitudinal
For example: Logistics	Convert entire product distribution fleet to electric vehicles	· Cost of vehicles · Reliability over long distances · Installation of on-site charging points · Staff resistance to change	· Financial · Logistical · Structural · Attitudinal

FIGURE 24 – Identifying Barriers Framework

Download the *Identifying Barriers* template at
sustainablebusinessbook.com.

ALL TALK, NO ACTION?
*Have you identified all the possible barriers
to progress?*

4.3. OVERCOME RESISTANCE

Resistance takes many forms. In electrical circuits, the term refers to the degree of opposition to the flow of a current. In human terms, it is the act or power of withstanding or opposing, sometimes using weapons. Without overdoing it on the military metaphor, all change (or transformation) programmes need to overcome this resistance in order to succeed.

The vital first step is to identify where the resistance is. Once these pain points have been recorded and agreed, you can set about creating a plan to overcome them. As ever, this requires brutal honesty and no artificial harmony. In other words, you can't deal with a problem if you won't admit it exists. Denial doesn't work. Once the barrier has been identified and named, you are halfway there. Choosing remedies and solutions is usually quite straightforward after that.

There are three main ways to navigate through areas of resistance, as shown in *Figure 25*.

- **Evasion (E):** If you are in a boat heading for a mine or rocks, then avoiding a collision is wise and essential. Use this approach for anything truly immovable.
- **Autocracy (A):** If you have unlimited authority, use it to remove the barrier completely.
- **Diplomacy (D):** A hybrid of the above, this method uses intelligent thinking to determine which battles are worth fighting in order to make progress. It is a little more circuitous perhaps, but pragmatic in the long run.

FIGURE 25 – Overcoming Resistance

Look at the method and start by identifying the business area, the proposed initiative and the main obstacle to getting it done, or potential barrier. Now build the case by defining the type of barrier, whose responsibility it is to deal with it and what needs to be addressed. Cement the plan by explaining how progress or success will be measured (*Figure 26*).

BUSINESS AREA	INITIATIVE	POTENTIAL BARRIERS	TYPE (E, A, D)
For example: Logistics	Fleet electrification	Staff resistance	Diplomacy

FIGURE 26 – Overcoming Resistance Framework

Download the *Overcoming Resistance* template at sustainablebusinessbook.com.

Measurement and personal responsibility are essential in this process. Without both, many best-laid plans simply never get done. Once a stance or initiative has been agreed, it needs to be decreed and enshrined in the constitution of the business. That means including sustainability metrics in the bonus structures so that incentives and rewards favour the right type of development and growth. It's human nature to pursue financial benefit, so you need to harness that emotion for the benefit of sustainable growth.

WHO IS RESPONSIBLE?	WHAT NEEDS TO BE ADDRESSED?	HOW WILL THIS BE MEASURED?
Dave, Head of Operations	Reliability of vehicles over long distances	Mileage proof and training

All of this adds up to commitments, not spreadsheets. There is no point in typing up huge lists of things to be done when they are going to languish somewhere in a drawer and never happen. The *Improvement Plan* must be a living, breathing, dynamic document – a constantly evolving statement that records effective progress.

ALL TALK, NO ACTION?
Have you identified all the different ways of overcoming resistance and your strategies for implementing them?

4.4. THE PURPOSE AND PROFIT CROSSOVER

Most businesses have never had a budget line dedicated to sustainability, so the idea of putting money behind it as a specific topic scares a lot of companies. The finance department doesn't like it and doesn't know where to allocate the cost. It's not just the cost of reengineering physical elements of the business – there is also the human resource required to make changes and get jobs done.

It may sound tough and it probably is, but you need to get used to it because the issue is not going to go away: **you need to generate a budget for your *Improvement Plan*.**

This means involving the money people from the off – whether that is your investors, your shareholders, your finance committee, a sceptical finance director or perhaps the head office in a global network.

Sustainability must build initiatives and programmes at the crossroads of *purpose* and *profit*.

What goes into a sustainability process is usually dozens of initiatives competing for resources. Nearly all will have solved a social or environmental need, but they should always be balanced with solving a business need. The moral is: don't suspend commercial questions early in the process. If you do, you will fall into the isolation trap (as in *Figure 27*).

The failure rate for sustainability programmes can be high, culminating in *unicorns* – visions that are lovely to think about but only doable and profitable in some imaginary world. What is needed is a pragmatic approach where the sustainability people *and* the commercial people work together from the off to solve both a big social or environmental problem *and* a big business problem in one bold move (as in *Figure 28*).

This two-sided thinking (sustainability need and company need) must be present from day one, because the best results appear at the crossroads of these two requirements.

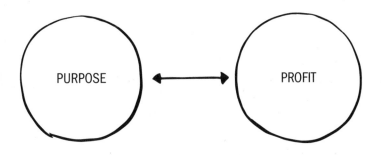

**FIGURE 27 – How *Not* to Approach Sustainability Investment –
The Isolation Trap**

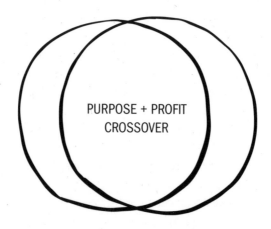

PURPOSE + PROFIT
CROSSOVER

FIGURE 28 – How to Approach Sustainability Investment Effectively

ALL TALK, NO ACTION?
*Have you addressed the issue of proper financial
commitment to your Improvement Plan?*

4.5. ANTICIPATE FIZZLE-OUT

Almost every initiative or project loses momentum at some point. It's human nature. We are very excited at the beginning but then the enthusiasm drops off. This can be described as the *motivational dip* (see *Figure 29*). The interesting thing is that this phenomenon can *always be predicted*. So there is no point in pretending that it won't happen. It is far more intelligent and effective to anticipate fizzle-out and build fail-safes into your plan from the start. Check-ins, reminders, incentives and sometimes even a quiet talking-to all play their part in keeping the plan on track. Be realistic about human motivation and get practical.

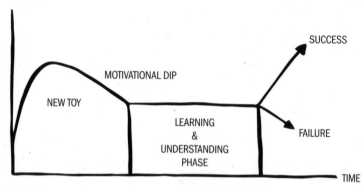

FIGURE 29 – The Motivational Dip

Sustainable commitment needs to run through the entire organization (see 3.4). Without robust and effective internal communication, principles can easily weaken in the face of day-to-day reality, as *Figure 30* nicely illustrates. This is often described as the *strategy/execution gap*.

Board enthusiasm means little if initiatives are met with cynicism on the front line. Strategies need to be fully explained to be successfully embraced at all levels of the business. Anticipate this and put measures in place to keep momentum going.

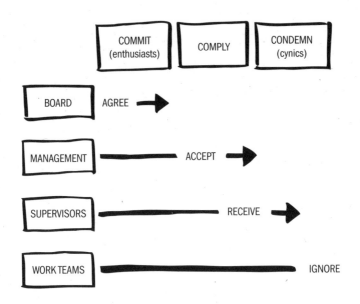

FIGURE 30 – Avoiding Fizzle-Out
Adapted from *Brand Manners*
(Hamish Pringle and William Gordon)

ALL TALK, NO ACTION?
Have you anticipated fizzle-out, predicted when this is likely to happen and discussed initiatives to keep momentum going?

IS THE BOARD ON BOARD?

It is time to overcome obstacles by:

- *Identifying barriers and overcoming resistance to progress*
- *Committing genuine financial and human resources*
- *Converting your Improvement Plan into achievable chunks*
- *Anticipating and preparing for loss of momentum and fizzle-out*

TO DO LIST

STAGE 3

ACTION

STEP FIVE – ENACT
GET IT DONE

The E of the PLANET System stands for **ENACT**.

Plans are pointless unless they get done. It requires constant effort and non-stop monitoring to make sure that things are on track.

This stage is not about sustainability in particular. It contains five provocations to jolt you and your team into actually getting things done.

If you are just talking, then you are not doing anything. So let's get on with it.

This stage provokes you into enacting everything you have decided on so far.

STEP FIVE
ENACT

5.1. DON'T CONFUSE DIRECTION WITH DESTINATION

Direction is a line or a course.

It goes a certain way, but, as you might have observed when looking at obstacles and how to overcome them, it's not the same as the destination (see 4.2).

Barely any journey, whether physical or temporal, follows a single straight line. Most involve a number of directions, plural. That's where the *Improvement Plan* comes in (see 3.5).

This is particularly true in the area of sustainability, since it is relatively new and information is constantly changing.

So your direction today may well be different from your direction tomorrow, even though the destination remains the same.

Smart businesspeople understand that different directions are needed to reach the ultimate destination. This is additionally complex and distracting when so many of the milestones you have set are so far in the future.

When pursuing the tasks on your *Improvement Plan*, never forget your true destination, and don't confuse it with your direction today (*Figure 31*).

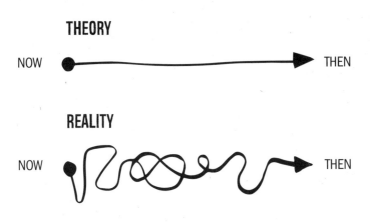

FIGURE 31 – Direction vs Destination

ALL TALK, NO ACTION?
Does everyone on the team understand your ultimate destination so that they can course correct as they go along?

5.2. ACT YOURSELF INTO A NEW WAY OF THINKING

People love sitting around talking about strategy.

It gives them an excuse to drink coffee and eat biscuits on company time.

But strategy is just a grand-sounding word for what you have decided to do, and it's especially convoluted when you are dealing with an infinite topic like sustainability.

Unless you get on and do it, by definition, you're still just talking.

There's an old academic joke: "Yes it works in practice, but does it work in theory?"

If your team or company spends too much time talking and not enough time doing, then they could do worse than heed this observation from Richard T. Pascale and Jerry Sternin writing in *Harvard Business Review*: "People are much more likely to act their way into a new way of thinking than think their way into a new way of acting."

In other words, once the thinking is done, stop talking and get on with it.

Then you'll really know if your idea works in practice.

This advice is a close cousin of the discipline known as *iterative testing*. Choose an approach that you believe will generate a sustainability quick win. Try it. Learn and adjust if necessary. Then repeat in a new iteration.

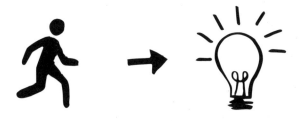

ALL TALK, NO ACTION?
Have you fooled yourself into believing that thinking is a substitute for doing?

5.3. STICK TO 20-MILE MARCHES

Polar explorer Roald Amundsen beat Captain Robert Scott to the South Pole by consistently marching 20 miles a day.

He had worked out in advance that 20 miles was the optimum (and sustainable) amount for a team with their equipment.

In bad weather the team did it anyway, and in good weather they stopped after 20 miles to save energy for the next day.

Scott's team either stayed in their tents on bad days or overshot on good ones and wore themselves out.

The moral is that companies, teams and individuals should aim for similar consistency.

This is what the business authors Jim Collins and Morten T. Hansen call *fanatic discipline* in their book *Great by Choice*.

Building a modern, resilient business is a many-headed beast. Sustainability projects are an infinite game. So it is very possible that you could overshoot on easier tasks and slow down horribly on harder ones.

Try not to do this. Don't ease off just because things are difficult or overdo it when things are easy.

Consistently do 20-mile marches and ask the same of your colleagues. This is another piece of brutal discipline that will counterbalance the challenge of heading towards milestones that are fiendishly difficult and far into the future.

It's tough, but it works.

ALL TALK, NO ACTION?
Have you implemented a measured and disciplined programme of effort?

5.4. PRECRASTINATE, DON'T PROCRASTINATE

Procrastination is a natural human trait. We put off things that are difficult to confront, hard to do or time-consuming (*Figure 32*).

The problem is that this doesn't work to our advantage at all. In fact, it usually makes things worse.

Many companies have delayed implementing their sustainability obligations for too long. One classic example is those that suddenly dive into panic mode when legislation is introduced that will jeopardize their business at a specific date in the very near future, sometimes threatening the entire existence of the company.

A much more intelligent approach is to *pre*crastinate. That means bringing forward more straightforward tasks and getting them done as efficiently and rapidly as possible, thereby reducing stress and liberating resources to do other things in the future (*Figure 33*).

This enables the team to celebrate mini-victories along the way, which keeps morale high and encourages momentum.

Those companies that just about limp over the line to meet a deadline imposed by some higher power are always on the back foot, which is bad for business. So don't do it.

Flying by the seat of your pants is never a good thing in business, so don't apply this lack of diligence to sustainability matters – just as you shouldn't to other tasks.

FIGURE 32 – Procrastination

FIGURE 33 – Precrastination

ALL TALK, NO ACTION?
Can you bring forward smaller or easier tasks?

5.5. PURSUE PROGRESS, NOT PERFECTION

Nothing is perfect, and yet any meeting or company will almost certainly include some people who claim to be perfectionists.

Some perfectionists are defensive and say they do it because no one else has standards as high as theirs.

But most perfectionists also confess that they do not like being that way, but strangely can't help it.

As we have established, becoming a company that has sustainability at its heart is not something that has a finite endgame. It's an infinite task and it's never done.

So, what to do?

Go for progress, not perfection.

This is not a euphemism or an excuse for low-quality work. It simply means that you should get on with it: 9 out of 10 will do. You can refine things later, but don't use the absence of the last 10% as an excuse to not implement an entire initiative.

Give it your best shot and then make it happen.

The planet doesn't care what is driving improvement, so long as improvement is made. Some improvement is always better than none.

And avoid criticizing others who aren't perfect (unless they are greenwashing – see 6.2). Everyone is on their own journey.

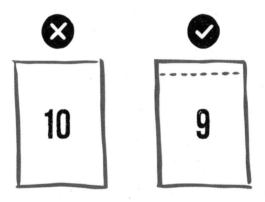

ALL TALK, NO ACTION?
Is perfectionism being used as an excuse not to launch an initiative?

IS THE BOARD ON BOARD?

It is time to get it done by:

- *Not confusing direction with destination*
- *Acting yourself into a new way of thinking*
- *Sticking to disciplined 20-mile marches*
- *Precrastinating not procrastinating*
- *Pursuing progress not perfection*

TO DO LIST

STEP SIX – TELL
COMMUNICATE
WITH INTEGRITY

The T of the PLANET System stands for **TELL**.

Finally, all of this work needs to be communicated authentically and intelligently to anyone who will listen – you need to **TELL** all your stakeholders: employees, shareholders, suppliers, customers and more.

This should only be done when you have set firm commitments in stone and already made real improvements.

This stage makes sure that you communicate everything you have done (and are doing) with honesty, humility and an appropriate tone. This applies equally to internal and external communications.

STEP SIX

TELL

6.1. MARKETING WITH A CONSCIENCE

If we look back over the years, there's little doubt that some blame can be placed at the door of marketing for its contribution to our current environmental and societal issues – from unhealthy lifestyles, obesity and debt to low self-esteem, poor mental health, materialism and general overconsumption.

Creative thinking and the art of persuasive communication have led many people to buy many products that they neither need nor really want.

But there is a big difference between marketers simply trying to do the best they can with a bad brief (or no brief) and marketers consciously manipulating the truth. Whatever the circumstances, the net result is that marketing helps companies sell more of their stuff (good or bad).

But marketers also have the skills to educate and encourage sustainable behaviour – from the boardroom to the shopping trolley – by clearly articulating the financial benefits of corporate sensitivity to people and the planet, and by championing the responsible use and disposal of products at the end of their life (or usefulness).

In order to do this, marketing needs to *become the conscience of the business* and a force for good, not just a PR tool.

An important role of a conscientious marketer is to understand and reflect the changing views and nature of target audiences. We have talked a little already about the rise in conscious consumerism – people wanting to be seen to be greener and using their purchasing power to buy goods and services that reflect their values and environmental sensitivity (see 1.3).

But it's not just full-on eco warriors you need to bear in mind. Companies may well be underestimating how many of their customers are only just starting to feel compromised by their current purchasing behaviour. The *conflicted consumer* sits somewhere between the ego warrior and the eco warrior (*Figure 34*). They appear to be extremely loyal – regularly purchasing products without, it would seem, any complaint. They like the quality, familiarity, price and convenience of a product but are conflicted about other more ethically dubious elements of the brand – anything from single-use plastic packaging to tax avoidance. The lack of a better alternative, however, keeps them coming back. The question is, for how long?

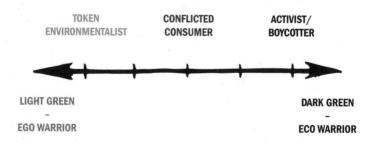

FIGURE 34 – Conflicted Consumerism

As these customers' environmental and societal awareness increases, so will their resentment at feeling that they have no option other than to buy an ethically questionable product or service.

The very moment a competitor brand matching yours for quality, price and convenience comes onto the market showing a clear purpose and commitment to better, more sustainable business practices, switching will be easy. And, even without this simple alternative, the longer the resentment builds, the more likely the customer will be to change their purchasing behaviour anyway, being unable to assuage their growing ethical conscience.

Marketing has a responsibility to recognize and understand these changing motivations. It should provide an invaluable feedback loop that helps ensure that sustainability issues are reported back to the board and therefore treated with the seriousness they deserve.

ALL TALK, NO ACTION?

Are you in touch with the changing motivations of your customers and does your marketing help educate and encourage sustainable behaviour?

6.2. BEWARE GREENWASHING

The term *greenwashing* was reportedly first used by an American environmentalist and researcher called Jay Westerveld. In 1986 he visited a beach resort in Samoa and was dismayed by the resort's claim that its innovative adoption of a reusable towel service was a way to *save the environment*. It was a classic overclaim – particularly since the resort was ambitiously expanding right next door in a highly non-environmentally friendly way.

Whitewashing: An attempt to stop people finding out the true facts about a situation.

Brainwashing: An attempt to make people believe something by repeatedly telling them that it is true and preventing any other information from reaching them.

Greenwashing: An attempt to make people believe that a company is doing more to protect the environment than it really is.

Whether mildly deceptive or intentionally manipulative, the term has now spawned many different variations (see the *Greenwashing Guide*).

Greenwashing is now rife. Brands use words to mislead, but also visuals and graphics. Green claims are often deceptively vague (and therefore unprovable). Many are overstatements or exaggerations about how environmentally friendly the product, company or service is. Some simply leave out or mask important information, using *selective transparency* and making a claim sound far better than it is.

One tactic is to use pseudo-scientific terms such as *eco* or *bio* – they sound impressive but in many cases are essentially meaningless. Another is a form of *symbolic corporate environmentalism*, which involves offering up seemingly impressive statistics that have been taken out of context. For example, Company X announces a $300 million investment in 'natural ecosystems' as part of a strategy to take action against climate change, while simultaneously investing $25 billion in non-renewable oil and gas energy sources.

With increased consumer scrutiny, more and more businesses are now being exposed for greenwashing. Sometimes, it is simply a case of perfectly good products that genuinely do help society or the planet using naive or lazy claims. At its worst, though, there are bad companies or brands (such as those directly involved with fossil fuels or deforestation) that use marketing claims to mislead and to make their product look acceptable.

In 2022, the Competition and Markets Authority in the UK introduced its Green Claims Code to help combat greenwashing. To avoid investigation, companies must be able to answer Yes to a series of questions, including:

- Are your claims clear and unambiguous?
- Do they only make fair and meaningful comparisons?
- Have you substantiated your claims (see 6.3)?

For more details, visit greenclaims.campaign.gov.uk.

The UK's Advertising Standards Authority has also published rules and guidance about misleading environmental advertising. For more details visit www.asa.org.uk.

ALL TALK, NO ACTION?
Are you guilty of symbolic corporate environmentalism, selective transparency or outright greenwashing?

6.3. CHECK, CLARIFY, CHALLENGE, CHANGE

It is natural for people to have an over-inflated view of their brand, product or service, especially if they work in the marketing department. Who wants a marketing director who doesn't think their product is great?

There are certainly many examples of premeditated and well-orchestrated greenwashing. But are the marketers always the villains here? Or is it sometimes simply a case of marketers being over-enthusiastic, grabbing at claims and terminology that their customers want to hear?

As custodians of a brand's reputation, marketers need to be wary and not become complicit in greenwashing – however attractive a claim may sound. Some simple cross-examination early on can flush out the dubious, the doubtful and the delusional.

The framework in *Figure 35* can help anyone interrogate a proposed marketing claim. It encourages communicators to look at the claim from a legal perspective (legally, can we say this?) *and* a moral perspective (okay, but morally, should we say this?).

If in any doubt, you need to:

- **CHECK** the facts
- **CLARIFY** the details
- **CHALLENGE** like (your greenest) customer
- **CHANGE** where necessary

Every claim, without exception, should be screened in this way.

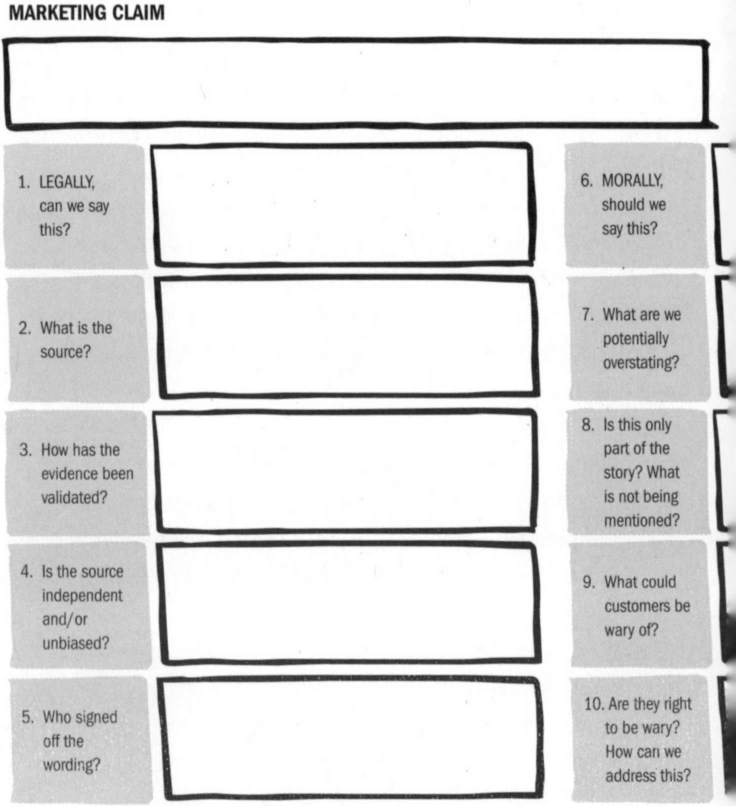

MARKETING CLAIM

1. LEGALLY, can we say this?		6. MORALLY, should we say this?
2. What is the source?		7. What are we potentially overstating?
3. How has the evidence been validated?		8. Is this only part of the story? What is not being mentioned?
4. Is the source independent and/or unbiased?		9. What could customers be wary of?
5. Who signed off the wording?		10. Are they right to be wary? How can we address this?

FIGURE 35 – Check, Clarify, Challenge, Change

ALL TALK, NO ACTION?

Are your marketing claims unrealistically enthusiastic and can they be properly substantiated?

GREENWASHING

What needs to be ......

CHECKED?

CLARIFIED?

CHALLENGED?

CHANGED?

"

He who is without carbon sin, cast the first lump of coal.

"

Mark Maslin, *How to Save Our Planet*

6.4. STAY HUMBLE

Embarking on a genuine sustainability journey is about understanding your impact on the world and taking significant steps to improve it. It is not about perfection. As we have said before, there is no such thing as a perfect corporation (see 5.5).

This is about acknowledging your imperfections and systematically addressing them.

Companies that shout too loudly and crow about their eco credentials in a smug, superior way will inevitably attract the sceptics. Even if they are not actually greenwashing, people may go digging for dirt and find enough to put them off purchasing.

It's much better to keep it real and involve your audience in the journey. Market with complete transparency. People will respect you and engage at a deeper level.

Every action has a reaction, and as you go along there is a high chance that you will make some mistakes. That's fine. The knack is to come clean and not try to hide them. You need to:

- Acknowledge misjudgements as soon as possible
- State exactly what happened
- Explain why the situation was tricky
- Outline what you have learned
- Clarify what you are doing about it

In many traditional forms of internal and external communication, the focus is on bigging up the company using evocative and promotional language.

By contrast, communicating sustainability with integrity requires a delicate balance between the heart and head – emotion and science. *But* the factual always needs to win out over the fanciful.

ALL TALK, NO ACTION?

Is your marketing humble enough to acknowledge imperfections, publicly explain mistakes and what you are doing to improve things?

6.5. REACT, REPORT, REPEAT

By following the PLANET System, you will now have stirred your company into action, agreed on your *Improvement Plan*, enacted some elements of the plan, and thought about how to communicate with integrity and without greenwashing.

There are many ways and places to communicate your new business approach, but a good start is to create an annual *Impact Report* (also called a sustainability or ESG Report). This should be done in the same way as you would publish a traditional annual report, and with the same degree of seriousness and authority. *Figure 36* outlines some of the areas you might want to consider communicating in your *Impact Report*.

WHAT'S DRIVING THIS?	Personal statement from the CEO: · Why you are doing this · How you plan to change (for good)
YOUR IMPACT	Statistics, insights and industry data Environmental and social impact evidence
YOUR SUSTAINABILITY JOURNEY	Overview of your long-term strategy
YOUR TOP 10 COMMITMENTS	Key actions and time frames
SUSTAINABLE DEVELOPMENT GOALS	How your strategy is aligned with global goals
BREAKING IT DOWN	This can cover: · Measuring your impact · Reducing your impact · Neutralizing or offsetting any residual impact · Managing your supply chain · Looking after your people · Understanding your customers · Caring for your communities · Promoting better business It can also include specific actions, initiatives, performance metrics and measurement criteria
CASE STUDIES	Spotlight on a couple of individual initiatives to help tell the story*
CERTIFICATION	Details of any certification or accreditation
SUSTAINABILITY PARTNERS	Who you are working with
ROAD MAP	Illustrating your journey so far and highlighting future commitments

FIGURE 36 – *Impact Report* Framework

*When we say "tell the story," we don't mean fanciful storytelling. This should be about initiatives that are well under way and can show proven results.

Incorporating a road map into the *Impact Report* is a neat way of illustrating your journey (*Figure 37*). On just one page, you can highlight your major achievements so far and show your future commitments – all in the form of milestones. If you have decided to align your sustainability plan with a net zero pathway, it is important here to add the specific (and measurable) reduction initiatives that will help you hit your 2030 and 2050 deadlines.

By the end of 2023
we will have ......

BY 2023

By 2030
we will have ......

BY 2030

By 2050
we will have ......

BY 2025

BY 2050

By August 2025
we will have ......

FIGURE 37 – Road Map

ALL TALK, NO ACTION?
Have you created an Impact Report framework and Road Map?

IS THE BOARD ON BOARD?

It is time to communicate with integrity by:

- *Making marketing the conscience of the business*
- *Avoiding greenwashing*
- *Checking, clarifying and challenging all claims*
- *Staying humble*
- *Reporting sustainability with the same authority and seriousness as the financials*
- *Publishing a Road Map with clear time-bound milestones*

TO DO LIST

ARE WE THERE YET?

It would be tempting to say that you have now reached the end of your journey. In a way you have, but the process never stops. Embedding sustainability into the fabric of your business requires a complete cultural change. Everyone in the organization needs to get into the habit of thinking differently.

Your *Improvement Plan* will inevitably need to be constantly updated. This is complex and you don't know what else will be discovered that could affect everyone's plans and best intentions. In turn, this will mean course correcting and updating customers, employees and partners – in real time with status reports, and then through your annual *Impact Report*.

We have outlined a system in this book to help give you structure, but the process of becoming a better and more resilient, responsible and sustainable business never ends (*Figure 38*).

Good luck with your efforts to improve your business. We can all help to make a difference.

sustainablebusinessbook.com

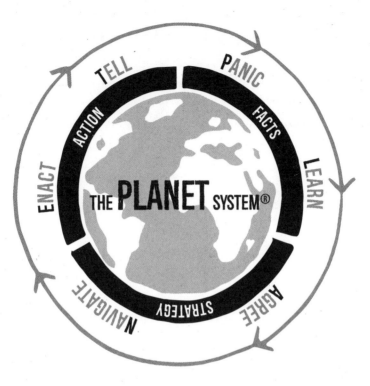

FIGURE 38 – The Perpetual PLANET System®

GREENWASHING GUIDE

2030 washing: Using the 2030 date to signal lofty ambitions and claims of improving a company's environmental record when in fact those bandying the date around have no intention of remaining in post to follow the promise through. For many, the date is so far in the future that they can reference it without revealing that they are in truth making little or no genuine progress to improve their activities.

Artwashing: Supporting the arts financially in order to disguise nefarious business dealings. This is a frequent complaint against many large corporations with questionable activities that attempt to improve their image by supporting art galleries, theatres and other artistic endeavours.

Bluewashing: Covering up unethical practices in relation to the sea, particularly fishing. Way behind the fossil fuel debate, many fail to understand the plunder of the oceans and the exploitative activities in which many companies indulge. This includes everything from inordinate levels of bycatch, poor or non-existent monitoring, misleading labelling and endorsement at point of sale, and even death of fisherman at sea. Many of these issues were exposed in the 2021 documentary *Seaspiracy*.

Causewashing: Touting a noble cause without following through with any authentic action. Companies and individuals can 'like' every charity cause possible on social media while simultaneously donating no time or money to help anybody or anything. This is self-glorification under the guise of good citizenship.

Coronawashing: Making a company look sympathetic to humanitarian causes while continuing corporate chicanery in the background. Cynical marketing departments spotted an opportunity to piggyback on phenomena such as Clap for Carers and the efforts of Captain Tom Moore to enhance their corporate reputations while simultaneously not changing their practices.

Diversish: Somewhat diverse, but not entirely so. As the diversity and inclusion agenda gains pace, many companies talk a good game on the topic but don't deliver. A classic example is when companies show encouraging data on the percentages of people employed by gender and ethnicity only for it to emerge that these people are all in lower-paid, more menial roles than all the white men in charge. There can also be wholesale disregard for groups that are differently abled.

Green hush: Total lack of comment on ethical matters by a company. This pair of words describes the complete absence of any communication or transparency from organizations whose predominant philosophy is to bury their heads in the sand and hope it all goes away.

Green sheen: Messaging gloss applied to corporate communications. This is usually broad-brush stuff designed to suggest that a company's activities are more ethical than they truly are.

Greenwashing: Pretending to be ethical when you are not. Usually considered to have developed out of the concept of whitewashing (attempting to stop people finding out the true facts about a situation).

Greenwishing: Hoping that a company's efforts will be seen in a favourable ethical light. This is an interesting take on (un)ethical activities in companies. Many are not that ethical but try to pretend that they are. Greenwishing has an element of hope about it, but in the wrong hands it is effectively equivalent to greenwashing.

Nicewashing: Making a company sound decent through appealing claims. These twee messages aim to disguise that the company is nothing of the sort. The messages are often a smokescreen of soft soap designed to conceal dubious working practices.

Purposewashing: Claiming that the purpose of a product, service or company is well intentioned when in fact it isn't. The classic smokescreen of any exploitative corporation: offering up a seemingly helpful image or social stance while simultaneously damaging the planet and its inhabitants behind the scenes.

Sportswashing: Sponsoring a popular sport or competition in order to soften or improve the image of a company. In extreme cases this can come close to money laundering as oligarchs channel earnings made from unethical businesses abroad into the purchase of, for example, Premier League football teams. Similar deals may be made by purchasers or sponsors from countries with unacceptable human rights records.

Wokewashing: When a company, institution or person says or does something that signals their support or sympathy for a marginalized cause while continuing to cause harm to vulnerable communities. Claiming one thing while doing another, this involves piggybacking on trendy issues to appear modern and relevant while not actually changing at all.

Unlike the rest of the book, this guide takes an irreverent and slightly cynical look at the various forms that greenwashing can take. For more examples of inappropriate marketing and misleading language, go to bulldictionary.com.

A–Z OF HELPFUL TERMS

All subjects have their jargon and acronyms. These plain English definitions should help you navigate the topic of sustainability with confidence.

Alt-proteins: *Alternative proteins, or meat alternatives, are plant-based or food-technology ('clean meat') alternatives to animal protein.*

Anthropocene: *The current geological age, viewed as the period in which human activity has been the dominant influence on climate and the environment.*

Biodegradable: *Capable of being decomposed by bacteria or other living organisms and thereby avoiding pollution.*

Biodiversity: *The variety of life on earth, including all plant and animal species.*

Biomass: *Plant or animal material used for energy production, or in industrial processes as a raw substance for various products. Types include purposefully grown energy crops, wood or forest residues, waste from food crops, horticulture, food processing, animal farming, and human waste from sewage plants.*

Biomimicry: *Emulating the models, systems and elements of nature to solve complex human problems.*

Carbon capture and storage (CCS): *The process of capturing and storing carbon dioxide before it is released into the atmosphere.*

Carbon credit: *A permit that allows a country or organization to produce a certain amount of carbon emissions that can be traded if the full allowance is not used.*

Carbon footprint: *The amount of carbon dioxide released into the atmosphere as a result of the activities of a particular individual, organization or community.*

Carbon neutrality: *Neutralizing carbon dioxide emissions by balancing them with removal elsewhere or eliminating them altogether.*

Carbon offsetting: *A way to neutralize or compensate for your carbon footprint by funding carbon reduction projects.*

Carbon tax: *Tax levied on the carbon content of fuels in sectors such as transport and energy. Carbon taxes aim to reduce carbon dioxide emissions by increasing the price of fossil fuels and decreasing the demand for them. They are a form of carbon pricing.*

Circular economy: *An economy based on the principles of designing out waste and pollution, keeping products and materials in use, and regenerating natural systems.*

Climate change: *A significant change in climate persisting over an extended period of time, typically for a number of decades or more.*

Climate crisis: *A headline descriptor for the threat of dangerous and irreversible changes to the world's climate.*

Climate positive: *A term used to describe activities that go beyond achieving net zero carbon emissions to create an environmental benefit by removing additional carbon dioxide from the atmosphere.*

Closed loop: *A system that does not accept inputs from, or create outputs to, any other system.*

CO_2 (carbon dioxide): *A naturally occurring gas in the earth's atmosphere. It is the main greenhouse gas released by human activities such as burning fossil fuels and biomass, industrial processes, and land-use change.*

CO_2e (carbon dioxide equivalent): *This covers all greenhouse gas emissions that contribute to climate change, including carbon dioxide (CO_2), methane (CH_4), nitrous oxide (N_2O) and refrigerant gases such as hydrofluorocarbons (HFCs). Some of these cause more global warming than others. Using CO_2e makes it easy to compare the impact of activities that emit different greenhouse gases. For example, 1 kg CH_4 = 25 kg CO_2e. This tells us that methane is 25 times more powerful as a greenhouse gas than carbon dioxide.*

Compostable: *Capable of being used as compost. Compostable materials are materials that break down completely into non-toxic components (water, carbon dioxide and biomass) that will not harm the environment.*

Conscious consumerism: *Increased consumer awareness of the impact of purchasing decisions on the environment and society.*

COP (Conference of Parties): *The governing body of an international convention – in this context, to discuss global climate change.*

Cradle to cradle: *A sustainable business strategy that mimics the regenerative cycle of nature in which waste is reused. Building on the cradle to grave approach of decreasing waste, cradle to cradle goes a step further and attempts to eliminate waste altogether.*

CSR (corporate social responsibility): *A management concept in which companies integrate social and environmental concerns into their business operations and interactions with suppliers and customers.*

Doughnut economics: *A visual framework for sustainable development – shaped like a doughnut – combining the concept of planetary boundaries with the complementary concept of social boundaries.*

Downstream emissions: *Emissions that occur in the life cycle of a material or product after its sale by the producer (including distribution and storage, use of the product and end of life).*

Earth Overshoot Day: *This marks the date each year when humanity has exhausted nature's budget for the year, as tracked by overshootday.org.*

Ecosystem: *A natural system consisting of all living organisms (plants, animals and microorganisms) in a specific area functioning together.*

Environmental footprint: *The effect that a person, company or activity has on the environment – for example, the amount of natural resources used and the amount of harmful greenhouse gases produced.*

ESG (environmental, social and governance): *The three central factors in measuring the sustainability and societal impact of business operations.*

Ethical: *Relating to beliefs about what is morally right and wrong.*

Fair trade: *The idea that producers in developing countries should be paid a fair price for their work by companies in developed countries. The price paid should provide enough for producers to afford essentials such as food, education and healthcare.*

Fossil fuels: *Fuels made from decomposing plants and animals. They are found in the earth's crust and contain carbon and hydrogen, which can be burned for energy. Examples include coal, oil and natural gas.*

Frugal innovation: *The process of reducing the complexity and cost of goods and their production. It usually refers to removing nonessential features from goods such as cars or mobile phones to sell them in developing countries. Also called frugal engineering.*

Global warming: *The gradual increase in the earth's average atmospheric and ocean temperatures.*

Good Life Goals: *Created by the World Business Council for Sustainable Development, these are 17 suggestions that explain how individuals can change their personal behaviour to help achieve the equivalent Sustainable Development Goals.*

Great Acceleration: *A term referring to the world's explosive growth since around the 1950s and, as a result, the unprecedented deterioration of the natural resources needed to fuel this growth.*

Green Claims Code: *Introduced in 2021 in the UK by the Competition and Markets Authority to combat corporate greenwashing (see greenclaims.campaign.gov.uk).*

Green growth: *A path of economic growth that uses resources in a sustainable way (unlike traditional economic growth, which typically does not account for environmental damage).*

Green recovery: *Packages of environmental, regulatory and fiscal reforms intended to recover prosperity in a responsible way after the Covid-19 pandemic.*

Greenhouse gases (GHGs): *Atmospheric gases of human or natural origin that absorb and emit heat. This results in heat being trapped in the climate system. The main greenhouse gases in the atmosphere are carbon dioxide, nitrous oxide, methane and water vapour.*

Greenwashing: *Making people believe that your company is doing more to protect the environment than it really is.*

Human capital: *Value derived from employees: physical presence, knowledge, skills, abilities, intellectual capacity, spirituality, empathy and passion.*

Impact investing: *Investments made with the intention of generating positive, measurable social and environmental impact as well as a financial return.*

Inertia principle: *A guiding principle of the circular economy, as introduced by Walter Stahel: "Do not repair what is not broken, do not remanufacture something that can be repaired, do not recycle a product that can be remanufactured. Replace or treat only the smallest possible part in order to maintain the existing economic value."*

LGBTQ+: *Acronym for lesbian, gay, bisexual, transgender, and queer or questioning. These terms are used to describe a person's sexual orientation or gender identity.*

Life cycle analysis: *A way of calculating the overall impact that a certain product has on the environment throughout its life.*

Linear economy: *A linear economy traditionally follows the take–make–use–waste plan. Raw materials are collected and transformed into products that are used until they are discarded as waste.*

Living wage: *A wage that is high enough to maintain a normal standard of living in the relevant country.*

Manufactured capital: *Infrastructure and tangible goods that an organization owns or leases to produce its outputs.*

Moral: *Relating to the standards of good behaviour, fairness and honesty that each person believes in, rather than to laws.*

Natural capital: *The world's stocks of natural assets, which include geology, soil, air, water and all living things. From natural capital, humans get food, drinking water, plants (for medicine, fuel and building materials), natural flood defences, carbon storage (e.g. peatlands), pollination of crops from insects and much more.*

Natural capitalism: *A global economic principle in which business and environmental interests overlap. It recognizes the interdependencies that exist between the production and use of human-made capital and flows of natural capital.*

Nature-based solutions: *The use of nature to jointly tackle social and environmental issues, such as climate change, food and water security, pollution and disaster risk – for example, reforestation to act as a natural carbon capture and storage facility.*

NDCs (nationally determined contributions): *Efforts or commitments made by countries to reduce their national emissions and adapt to the impacts of climate change.*

Net zero: *A state in which the activities of a company or country result in no net impact on the climate from greenhouse gas emissions. This is achieved by reducing emissions to zero or counterbalancing their effect with an appropriate amount of carbon removal elsewhere in the business (or country).*

Organic: *Relating to or derived from living matter.*

Paris Agreement: *A United Nations convention on climate change, signed in 2016, that aimed to deal with greenhouse gas emissions. Sometimes referred to as the Paris Accord.*

Planetary boundaries: *A set of nine parameters within which humanity can develop and thrive for generations to come, so long as they are not exceeded.*

Recycling: *The action or process of converting waste into reusable material.*

Reforestation: *The natural or intentional restocking of existing forests and woodlands (forestation) that have been depleted, usually through deforestation.*

Remanufacturing: *Manufacturing an old product into a new product.*

Repurposing: *Finding a new use for an idea, product or building.*

Science-Based Targets initiative (SBTi): *This champions science-based target-setting to boost companies' competitive advantage in the transition to the low-carbon economy. It is a collaboration between the Carbon Disclosure Project, the United Nations Global Compact, the World Resources Institute and the World Wide Fund for Nature.*

Scope 1: *The GHG Protocol Corporate Standard's term for direct emissions from owned or controlled sources.*

Scope 2: *The GHG Protocol Corporate Standard's term for indirect emissions from the generation of purchased energy.*

Scope 3: *The GHG Protocol Corporate Standard's term for all non-Scope 2 indirect emissions that occur in the value or supply chain, including both upstream and downstream emissions.*

Stakeholder: *In a corporation, a stakeholder is a member of a group without whose support the organization would cease to exist.*

Sustainable: *Able to continue over a period of time. In relation to the environment, it means causing little or no damage to the environment and therefore able to continue for a long time.*

Sustainable Development Goals (SDGs): *The 17 goals adopted by all United Nations member states in 2015 as a universal call to action to end poverty, protect the planet, and ensure that all people enjoy peace and prosperity by 2030 (see un.org/sustainabledevelopment).*

Tipping point: *The critical point in a situation, process or system beyond which a significant and often unstoppable effect or change takes place.*

Upcycling: *Also known as creative reuse, this is the process of transforming by-products, waste materials or unwanted products into new materials or products perceived to be of greater quality – often through adding artistic or environmental value.*

Upstream emissions: *Emissions that occur during the life cycle of a material or product up to the point of sale by the producer (including all the raw materials, transportation of those materials to assembly or manufacturing, and business travel).*

Zero-to-landfill: *The most common interpretation of this concept is that at least 99% of generated waste is diverted away from landfill. This means that all waste produced is reused, recycled, composted or sent to energy recovery. The Carbon Trust has developed a zero-to-landfill certification programme.*

REFERENCES, RESOURCES AND FURTHER READING

The body of literature on ethical and sustainable business practice is growing steadily. One-page summaries can be found at ethicalbusinessblog.com. Do check back regularly as this library will continue to be updated after the publication of this book.

5 Reasons Why We Need to Reduce Global Inequality (blog post, World Economic Forum, 2015)

50 Ways to Help the Planet, Sian Berry (Kyle Books, 2018)

A Life on Our Planet, David Attenborough (Witness Books, 2020)

A Safe and Just Space for Humanity, Kate Raworth (discussion document, Oxfam, 2012)

All In, David Grayson, Chris Coulter and Mark Lee (Routledge, 2018)

Authentic Marketing, Larry Weber (John Wiley, 2019)

Better, John Grant (Unbound, 2018)

Brand Manners, Hamish Pringle and William Gordon (Wiley, 2003)

Business Ethics, Andrew Crane, Dirk Matten, Sarah Glozer and Laura Spence (Oxford University Press, 2016)

Clever, Rob Goffee and Gareth R. Jones (Harvard Business Review Press, 2009)

Climate Change: A Very Short introduction, Mark Maslin (Oxford University Press, 2021)

Climate Change and the Road to Net Zero, Mathew Hampshire-Waugh (Crowstone Publishing, 2021)

Compassion Inc, Gaurav Sinha (Ebury Press, 2018)

Conscious Capitalism Field Guide, Raj Sisodia, Timothy Henry and Thomas Eckschmidt (Harvard Business Review Press, 2018)

Conscious Leadership, John Mackey, Steve McIntosh and Carter Cripps (Portfolio Penguin, 2020)

Diversify, June Sarpong (HQ, 2017)

Doughnut Economics, Kate Raworth (Random House, 2017)

Drive, Daniel Pink (Canongate, 2011)

Eating the Big Fish, Adam Morgan (John Wiley, 1999)

Economics for a Fragile Planet, Edward Barbier (Cambridge University Press, 2022)

Engaging for Success: Enhancing Performance through Employee Engagement, David Macleod and Nita Clarke (report to government, 2012)

Ethical Marketing and the New Consumer, Chris Arnold (John Wiley, 2009)

False Alarm, Bjorn Lomborg (Basic, 2020)

Frugal Innovation, Navi Radjou and Jaideep Prabhu
(Profile Books, 2016)

Good Is the New Cool, Afdhel Aziz and Bobby Jones
(Regan Arts, 2016)

Great by Choice, Jim Collins and Morten T. Hansen
(Random House, 2011)

Green Swans, John Elkington (Fast Company Press, 2020)

Greener Marketing, John Grant (Wiley, 2020)

How to Avoid a Climate Disaster, Bill Gates (Allen Lane, 2021)

How Bad Are Bananas?, Mike Berners-Lee (Profile, 2020)

How to Kill a Unicorn, Mark Payne (Nicholas Brealey, 2014)

How to Save Our Planet, Mark Maslin (Penguin Life, 2021)

Humane Capital, Vlatka Hlupic (Bloomsbury, 2019)

Millennial Employee Engagement Study
(Cone Communications, 2016)

Natural Capital, Dieter Helm (Yale University Press, 2015)

Net Positive, Paul Polman and Andrew Winston (Harvard Business
Review Press, 2021)

Net Zero, Dieter Helm (William Collins, 2020)

No Bullshit Leadership, Chris Hirst (Profile Books, 2019)

No One Is Too Small to Make a Difference, Greta Thunberg
(Penguin, 2019)

Our Final Warning, Mark Lynas (4th Estate, 2020)

Speed & Scale, John Doerr (Penguin Business, 2021)

Sustainable Business: A One Planet Approach, Sally Jeanrenaud, Jean-Paul Jeanrenaud and Jonathan Gosling (John Wiley, 2016)

Sustainable Marketing, Michelle Carvill, Gemma Butler and Geraint Evans (Bloomsbury, 2021)

The Ethical Business Book, Sarah Duncan (LID, 2021)

The Ethical Capitalist, Julian Richer (Random House, 2018)

The Ethical Leader, Morgen Witzel (Bloomsbury, 2018)

The Five Dysfunctions of a Team, Patrick Lencioni (John Wiley, 2002)

The Future We Choose, Christiana Figueres and Tom Rivett-Carnac (Manilla Press, 2020)

The Infinite Game, Simon Sinek (Penguin, 2019)

The Joy of Work, Bruce Daisley (Random House, 2019)

The Joyful Environmentalist, Isabel Losada (Watkins, 2020)

The New Brand Spirit, Christian Conrad and Marjorie Ellis Thompson (Gower Publishing, 2013)

The New Climate War, Michael E. Mann (Scribe, 2021)

The New Rules of Green Marketing, Jacquelyn Ottman (Greenleaf, 2010)

The Performance Economy, Walter Stahel (Palgrave Macmillan, 2010)

The Pirate Inside, Adam Morgan (John Wiley, 2004)

The Sales Person's Secret Code, Ian Mills, Mark Ridley, Ben Laker and Tim Chapman (LID, 2017)

The Sustainable Business, Jonathan T. Scott (Greenleaf, 2013)

The Sustainable Business Handbook, David Grayson, Chris Coulter and Mark Lee (Kogan Page, 2022)

The Troubling Evolution of Corporate Greenwashing, Bruce Watson (The Guardian, 2016)

The Uninhabitable Earth, David Wallace-Wells (Allen Lane, 2019)

There Is No Planet B, Mike Berners-Lee (Cambridge University Press, 2019)

Volt Rush, Henry Sanderson (Oneworld, 2022)

We Are the Weather, Jonathan Safran Foer (Penguin, 2019)

WEconomy, Craig Kielburger, Holly Branson and Marc Kielburger (John Wiley, 2018)

What If Solving the Climate Crisis Is Simple?, Tom Bowman (Changemaker Books, 2020)

Who Cares Wins, David Jones (Pearson, 2012)

Why Should Anyone Work Here?, Rob Goffee and Gareth Jones (Harvard Business Review Press, 2015)

Your Company's Secret Change Agents, Richard T. Pascale and Jerry Sternin (Harvard Business Review, 2005)

Asa.org.uk

BetterBusinessAct.org

BCorporation.net

CarbonTrust.com

Defra.gov.uk

EllenMacarthurFoundation.org

EthicalConsumer.org

ExponentialRoadmap.org

GHGProtocol.org

GreenClaims.Campaign.gov.uk

GoodBusinessCharter.com

GreenkeyEngland.co.uk

HeyGirls.co.uk

PlanetMark.com

Pledge1Percent.org

Mindfulchef.com

OnePercentForThePlanet.org

ScienceBasedTargets.org

TheSRA.org

UN.org/SustainableDevelopment

WBCSD.org

SPECIAL THANKS

Zoe Bale, Mike Berners-Lee, Richard Bradford, Jamila Brown, Gemma Butler, Louise Carr-Merino, Nigel Clarkson, Shaunagh Duncan, Tim Etherington-Judge, Dave Hart, David Hill, Oliver Joyce, Kalindi Juneja, Stephan Loerke, Alastair Maxwell, Rachel Maxwell, Danny Pecorelli, Jane Pendlebury, Chris Pike, Simon Rhind-Tutt, Laura Schacht, Gillian Tett, Cecilia Weckstrom and Sue Williams.

ABOUT THE AUTHORS

KEVIN DUNCAN is a business adviser, marketing expert, motivational speaker and author. After 20 years in advertising, he has spent the last 22 as an independent troubleshooter, advising companies on how to change their businesses for the better.

SARAH DUNCAN is a sustainability consultant and educator with over 30 years of business experience. She helps organizations understand the commercial and moral benefits of ethical and responsible business practice.

Contact the authors for advice and training:
kevinduncanexpertadvice@gmail.com
sarah@sleepinglion.co.uk
expertadviceonline.com
sleepingliononline.com
sustainablebusinessbook.com

ALSO BY THE AUTHORS IN THE CONCISE ADVICE SERIES

The Bullshit-Free Book
The Business Bullshit Book
The Diagrams Book
The Ethical Business Book
The Excellence Book

The Ideas Book
The Intelligent Work Book
The Smart Strategy Book
The Smart Thinking Book

The Ethical Business Book and *The Smart Strategy Book* are ideal companions to this one. Find out more at ethicalbusinessblog.com and thesmartstrategybook.com.

ISBN: 978-1-911687-52-8

ISBN: 978-1-911687-22-1

ISBN: 978-1-911687-53-5

ISBN: 978-1-911498-51-3

ISBN: 978-1-911671-50-3

ISBN: 978-1-910649-85-5

ISBN: 978-1-911687-54-2

ISBN: 978-1-912555-70-3

ISBN: 978-1-911687-80-1

NOTES

NOTES